D0947715

JOAN & GOODRIDGE

Joan and Goodridge, Milan, 1954.

Joan & Goodridge

My Life with Goodridge Roberts

Joan Roberts

Véhicule Press

Published with the generous assistance of The Canada Council for the Arts, the Book Publishing Industry Development Program of the Department of Canadian Heritage, and the Société de développement des entreprises culturelles du Québec (SODEC).

Cover design: J.W. Stewart
Cover painting, "Girl in Black, 1959" (Joan Roberts) by Goodridge Roberts, courtesy of Glynnis French
Colour plates photographed by Sun Knudsen
Special thanks: Bob Tombs
Set in Minion by Simon Garamond
Printed by Marquis Printing Inc.

Copyright © Joan Roberts 2009
All rights reserved.

LIBRARY AND ARCHIVES CANADA CATALOGUING IN PUBLICATION DATA

Roberts, Joan, 1922-
Joan & Goodridge : my life with Goodridge Roberts/
Joan Roberts
ISBN 978-1-55065-262-8
1. Roberts, Joan, 1922-. 2. Roberts, Goodridge, 1904-1974.
3. Painters' spouses—Canada—Biography.
4. Women social workers—Quebec (Province)—Montreal—
Biography. I. Title.

ND249.R6R632009   759.11   C2009-903492-1

Published by Véhicule Press, Montréal, Québec, Canada
www.vehiculepress.com

Distribution in Canada by LitDistCo
www.litdistco.ca

Distributed in the U.S. by Independent Publishers Group
www.ipgbook.com

Printed in Canada on recycled paper

Contents

List of Colour Plates

Preface

WHEN GOODRIDGE ROBERTS and I met, he was forty-eight and I was thirty. It was 1952 and he was beginning to be recognized as one of Canada's most important artists. He had been chosen to represent Canada along with Alfred Pellan, Emily Carr, and David Milne in Canada's first inclusion in the Venice Biennale in 1952 and in the same year he represented Canada at the Carnegie International in Pittsburgh.

My initial motivation in writing this book was to tell the story of our life together and to add my recollections to the information about him that has appeared in other publications. I began writing in the 1980s, recording my memories of our summer at Bonnie Isle in Pointe au Baril and later that year in Fredericton. Early readers of the fragments were supportive and urged me on. Even with their approval I found it difficult to continue because I had kept myself out of the story and this gave a lopsided picture of Goodridge's life in those days. I put aside writing anything further for a long period.

When I began taking courses at the McGill Centre for Learning in Retirement in 2002, I began with the group entitled "Write Your Life" under the neutral and dispassionate eye of Mebbie Aikens with no clear linkage in my mind to the material I had already produced. I wrote brief new episodes that were as unrevealing as possible about who the characters actually were. The process, however, did get me writing again although I was still unsure where I was going. Another pause ensued but then in the autumn of 2005 I answered an advertisement in the newspaper for a memoir writing group that would use themes and related questions provided by the leader, Katherine Akerley. Our small group lasted more than a year under her encouraging leadership and was another opportunity to hone my writing ability and clarify where this project should go.

In 2008 I worked steadily with Wendy Scott, who helped me to fit the pieces together, to give shape to the material. I thank her for her skilful expertise in helping bring this book to fruition.

Charlie Hill, Curator of Canadian Art at the National Gallery of Canada, kindly gave me access to the Dominion Gallery archives located there and Cindy Campbell was most helpful in locating relevant material for me.

Both before and during the writing of this book, my friends have taken on a large importance in my life both for companionship and counsel. In addition to those later named in the story, others have been crucial in my life. Bill and Gladys Kinnis, Phyllis Poland and then Dorothy Sirota and Betty Ann Affleck belong to the early years of my trying to cope alone. Barbara Nichols and Claire Helman participated in the genesis of the idea of a book and have never wavered in their support of my project. I owe them a great deal though they must not be reproached for its deficiencies. Shirley Steele, Liesel Urtnowski, Mimi Caouette, Phyllis Amber, Florence Stevens and others have encouraged me in my struggles and remain important to me. Peter Haynes and Bob Tombs helped me navigate to a publisher, a world with which I was utterly unfamiliar. Both Nancy Marrelli and Simon Dardick of Véhicule Press have given me unending help and attention.

Finally I want to underline the phenomenal support and acceptance of both my children, Tim and Glynnis, to whom this book is dedicated with a great deal of love. It would not have happened without their encouragement and I hope they feel the result pleases them and justifies their support.

CHAPTER ONE

Beginnings: Toronto

THE TORONTO WHERE I WAS BORN in 1922 and where I lived for twenty-one years was so unlike the Toronto of today that it is hard to believe it is the same city. At that time nearly all of its citizens were white and of British descent. Their views were conservative, predictable, often narrow, and social behaviour was so rigid and conformist that the morals and attitudes of today's generation would have been unimaginable to them.

Compared to other families of that period, ours was small. I was a middle child, five years younger than my sister Mary and three years older than my brother John. Mother's first baby was a stillborn boy. Mary's safe arrival four years later had been followed by the birth of another boy who lived for only a year and a half. I knew nothing about the circumstances of his death but this did not stop me from imagining what it might have been like to have a brother just a bit older, particularly as adolescence approached. I was sure that he would have eased my way into the world of boys, and would have had friends who liked me. In my eyes John was much too young to play that role and was only good for me to tease. I do not know how the losses of two of her babies affected my mother, but I did wonder later if they were part of the reason that when I was an infant she could not nurse me but used a breast pump, apparently because I was not willing to take milk from her.

When I was two years old we moved into a fine, newly-built

three-storey house at 124 Lawrence Crescent in North Toronto, right at the edge of the city, with fields behind it and few other houses on the street. This good fortune came about because my middle name was Carruthers, given to me by mother, Margaret Belle Haig, after her Scottish relatives. My parents were able to buy the house when her cousin, James Carruthers, a wealthy grain merchant living in Montreal, died and left her approximately $18,000 in his will because of her fortunate choice of Carruthers for my middle name.

Our new house stood on a large lot that sloped away at the rear, landscaped into three terraces. On the top terrace we had our sand-box in the summer, while during some winters there was a fine skating rink built by our father. Everyone helped to keep it free of snow so it could be used to practice the figures and jumps we learned at the Toronto Skating Club. On the second level were a couple of pear trees and four rose beds tended by my dad who was an avid rose gardener. The bottom terrace, the largest, was where each of us had our own wildflower garden and where we played badminton.

Every fall on a weekend Dad would take over the two laundry tubs in the basement and fill them with cut-up vegetables to make mustard pickles bottled for the winter. Pickled pears were another of his impressive culinary accomplishments, a product of his child-hood on a farm in the rural Ontario village of Elora.

As far as parenting was concerned, I often got the feeling that my parents had solved all the difficult questions of life because they seemed to have a maxim for every occasion. Wrestling with difficult moral issues? Trying to imbue the children with values that would become the core of their personalities? There seemed to be a proverb that fit every situation and it was presented as an immutable truth. An attraction to something they disapproved of would quickly elicit "All that glitters is not gold." Finding it hard to get going would produce the caution "The early bird gets the worm." A tendency to blame others for one's shortcomings was nipped in the bud with "People in glass houses should not throw stones." An impending decision might produce "Don't throw the baby out with the bath water," and bad fortune was tempered with "Every cloud has a silver lining." These perhaps took the place of strong religious injunctions and prohibitions.

Our mother, like most wives and mothers of the time, did not work outside the house, and we all looked forward to Dad's arrival home at the end of the day. I adored him and vied to be his favourite child. After his death, my mother told me, "You know, you were his favourite," and suddenly conscious of all the effort I had expended to win his approval, my reply was, "Why did he never tell me?"

In my adult years I realized how much I did not learn from my mother and how helpful it would have been if she had been able to be more forthcoming. Information on menstruation consisted of an advertising booklet left casually where I might see it. Mother was too shy to mention sex when I was an adolescent. All my knowledge came bit by bit from girlfriends or books I read as a teenager such as *Testament of Youth* by Vera Brittain or even Thomas Hardy's *Tess of the d'Urbervilles.*

When I think back, it is my father, Fredric Charteris Carter, who emerges as the central person in our lives. He was a corporate lawyer, a partner in a large downtown firm. Perhaps because most of our childhood occurred during the Great Depression and there was less business at his law firm, or perhaps because life was more leisurely in those days, he spent a lot of time doing things with us children. He taught us to ski at the Rosedale Golf Club, skated with us on the backyard rink or at the Friday afternoon dances at the Toronto Skating Club, and always came to the school to see us on Field Days. Both Mary and I partici-pated for a number of years in the three-night annual figure skating carnivals put on by the Toronto Skating Club at Maple Leaf Gardens. I moved up from a tin soldier to the Junior Ballet, but my most exciting moment was getting the autograph of Sonja Henie, the European figure skating champion who was a star feature one year. I remember vividly how I once painfully concealed the fact that a chicken pox pustule had broken out on my foot. Although I could barely walk, never mind skate, I couldn't bear the thought of missing the night's magic.

Mother played a less active role in our lives. She passed along her love of music to us, but not domestic skills. She did not like to cook herself, so she did not spend time or effort teaching Mary or me. Instead, we always had a young country girl living in the house. Times were hard in the '30s, so it was always easy to find a young girl who had come into the city from the country and who was glad to do the cooking and housework for room and board and twenty dollars a month. We grew very fond of some of these girls, and they became an integral part of our family life, sometimes staying with us for years.

The long years of our childhood passed happily, with each year sharply divided between summer and the rest of the year. From fall to spring the days were filled with school, which I always loved, with music and skating lessons, Sunday school, and wild Westerns at the local movie theatre on Saturday afternoons made even better with a few cents' worth of carefully chosen penny candy. Life on our street included games, bicycles, and most exciting, the digging and building of forts undergound in vacant lots which we furnished with whatever we could scrounge. I think I received my first non-familial kiss down there at eight or nine years old. How I hated having to leave an exciting game of Run Sheep Run to go inside when it grew dark! The most distressing event I can remember from that time was skidding on my bicycle when Mount Pleasant Avenue had been freshly oiled, ruining a new dress, and being afraid to confess this to my mother. Every spring the unpaved dirt roads were covered with old black oil to keep the dust down, and for the first few days they were as slick as a skating rink.

Summers meant our beloved Wawanaissa Island on Georgian Bay, where we joined relatives and friends for the holidays. Our connection to the area goes back to 1908, when my father and a fellow university student in Toronto decided to spend their summer vacation camping and canoeing at Pointe au Baril. I am not sure they knew at the time that Samuel de Champlain had preceded them there by three hundred years. This was the start of a deep love for the Bay that has continued in our family to this day. I have spent nearly every summer of my life there, and its rugged beauty of rocks, water, islands, and pines has etched itself into my heart and psyche. I believe, in fact, that in many ways it has helped to form my character. To the times I spent there I owe much of my independent spirit, my fortitude, my stamina and tenacity, and whatever creativity and ingenuity I may possess. Over the years I have seen many others succumb to its peaceful, pleasing arrangement of forms where a few yards can alter totally a pattern of rock, juniper bushes, and pines. The eye is never sated by this landscape, where a sense of endurance persists in the ancient rocks and pines leaning away from the prevailing west wind as they cling to a speck of earth in a rock fissure. In an instant, change can occur as a sudden thunderstorm or wind storm whips up the waves in the open bays. An islander never loses entirely the awareness that danger may erupt without any warning. In those early years, since nearly all the islands belonged to the Crown and were uninhabited, one could camp anywhere and enjoy the feeling of owning the world, even if replenishing food supplies involved paddling ten or more miles.

Before they were married, my parents spent a summer there camping—a type of accommodation that had many drawbacks, particularly for my mother. She often described how she felt when she learned she had to throw out all metal objects from the tent in a lightning storm. She was even more chagrined when my father told her next morning that the cot she had been sleeping on was made of iron. Later, when they had a little more money, my parents rented various cottages in the area, and then finally, in 1922, they bought the island, later christened Wawonaissa ("whippoorwill" in Ojibwa) with some of their relatives, and built upon it. The property consisted of six or seven acres but it seemed a vast area when I was a child. I remember being in bed in the city during the winter, trying to reconstruct in my mind's eye the exact footsteps I would take along the rough path from the main house to the boathouse at the back of the island. I could never make it the whole way before I fell asleep.

I recall my great (and selfish) joy in the 1930s when a polio epidemic in Toronto kept the schools closed into September and we stayed longer at the cottage. There, a holiday atmosphere always seemed to prevail. It overflowed with various family members and friends, so there were no dull or lonely moments. We children were provided with a learning environment in which we mastered all sorts of outdoor skills—although one athletic feat I failed to master, to my dismay, was to chin myself with one hand on the bar in the doorway. My inspiration for this feat was Napoleon, an Indian fishing guide and our full-time helper during one or two of our summers there.

As soon as we learned to swim, we spent hours playing in the water, exulting in the freedom of unlimited time and space, and in handling the canoes and rowboats. Indoors, together with the adults, we held contests in writing poems, composing and singing songs, and performing short plays, as well as the usual card and board games and jigsaw puzzles. As a teenager I participated in the area's annual regattas by taking part in the swimming, canoeing, and diving competitions. By this time there were enough cottagers on the islands to make this possible, and a volunteer spirit strong enough to make any project run successfully.

As I look back to my childhood, it seems to stretch out into long, uneventful years that went by in more or less the same way. Three events occurred during the '30s that proved to be turning points, however: having to change schools because of money problems, going to England for the coronation of King George VI, and my father's death, when I was fifteen.

[top] The family. From left, John, Joan, Mary, Mother, Dad.
[bottom] Joan, John, and dog Fluffy, c. 1929.

[top] Early Georgian Bay picnic with Mother and Dad (at right), C. 1915.
[bottom] Back row: Aunt Allie, Aunt Nana, Noel Charteris, Dad (Fredric
Carter), John Charteris (Noel's husband–both visiting cousins from
Britain), Mother (Margaret Carter). Front row: Mary and Joan, 1937.

In 1931 I was nine years old. Canada was in the throes of the Great Depression. Thousands were out of work and there were hunger marches on Ottawa, relief camps, and great suffering for many families. Although business at my father's law firm undoubtedly dwindled, we were never really in want. (The ten-pound tins of broken biscuits Dad brought to the island each summer hardly belied our privileged economic status.) I did not fully understand why strange men would come to our door asking for food, or work they might do. At one point we were given an address some blocks away to which we would send them, but I never had much faith they would get anything there.

It came as a great shock when my parents told me I would have to leave Havergal College, the private girls' school I was attending, and transfer to the nearest public school. I had been happy where I was, and what lay ahead was unknown. What stands out from that time was the reaction of my teacher when, much to my surprise, she began to cry at the thought of losing me. I was puzzled and perturbed, and I recall the feeling of discomfort her display of emotion gave me. Two years later, when my father's improving financial situation allowed me to return to my all-girls school, I was as reluctant to return as I had been to leave. By this time boys of course had become the big attraction. I stayed at Havergal until my high-school graduation and am very grateful for both the intellectual aspects and the emphasis on learning to play a variety of games and sports, that combined to give me competencies and self-confidence.

The second event occurred in 1937, when one day the school announced that the National Education Association was planning to send 300 Canadian schoolchildren to London for the forthcoming coronation of King George VI. Of the 150 girls and 150 boys representing all parts of the Dominion, two would be chosen from our school. Those applicants who were selected would only have to pay $250 and supply their own pocket money for the nine weeks in England. I was fourteen years old, in Secondary Three, and therefore freer to be away in May and June than the older students, who would have to be in Ontario to write their matriculation examinations for university entrance, and I was chosen from my school. My parents decided to use the occasion for a trip there as well, and although I only saw them for a day or two, it was comforting to know they were nearby as the visit progressed, particularly when homesickness struck. I still possess a letter from my father reminding me, in kindly but rather clichéd terms, that although I might be feeling downcast, every cloud has a silver lining.

Like most Ontario Anglos at the time, I was a confirmed monarchist and supporter of the British Empire. Whenever British Royalty visited Toronto, the family would always be there to wave enthusiastically from the curb as the royal carriage passed by. Deep down, a large majority of English Canadians felt that England was still the homeland, the Old Country, and Canada a mere colony, so the opportunity to actually visit there for the coronation seemed unusually fortuitous.

I kept a diary of the trip, and reading it now I marvel at my naïveté and enthusiasm. We crossed the Atlantic on the *Duchess of Athol*, and it hardly seemed to matter that we were four persons and eight suitcases in a 7 x 7-foot cabin, or that it was April, and the weather on the North Atlantic was grey, cold, and windy. A chief preoccupation was the difficulty of having a bath. Bath times came rarely and were scheduled, often for very inconvenient times. There was not a lot to do during the eight-day voyage, but we wrote many letters, saw several movies, and made new friends and alliances that seemed very important at the time.

Had my trip ended just after the ocean voyage it still would have been the most exciting thing that had ever happened to me. But then we arrived, and everything about England seemed new and different: the trains, the money, the accents of the people, the neat, clipped hedges instead of fences, the brilliant green of the countryside. During our two weeks in London we stayed at the Y.W.C.A. on

Great Russell Street. There we learned to sing "Oh Canada" in both languages, to sing the hymn "Jerusalem", and to improve our rendition of "God Save the King". We assembled at the Royal Albert Hall for a huge Youth Rally where young people from all over the world came to sing. We visited important historic sites including the Tower of London, the Parliament Buildings, Westminster Abbey, Kew Gardens, and Hampton Court. After a while we were allowed to wander around London unsupervised and this gave us a great feeling of freedom and of being grown up.

Finally the day of the coronation arrived. London was gaily decorated for the occasion and the excitement and tension were palpable everywhere. We were awakened before 3 a.m. for toast and marmalade, then began the long walk to the stands with a guide who had studied the traffic patterns of the route we were to take. Our pre-arranged seats were near Buckingham Palace, where the procession would be visible both going to and returning from Westminster Abbey.

As the lights started to come on in the Palace, cars containing foreign royalty appeared, followed by horses and carriages carrying prime ministers and soldiers in all kinds of dazzling uniforms. The colour, pomp, and pageantry were electrifying. Nowadays it is hard to imagine or to recall how important such a visual experience was in those days before television, which brings events to the world as they occur. Then, one had to be present to get the full impact of such an event. After the ceremony, so reluctant were we to have it all over, that we waited a long time in the rain to see the new King and Queen come out on the balcony of the palace to wave to the crowd.

For three weeks of the trip, we were sent in twos and threes to different boarding schools to learn what an English student experience was like. I was sent to Cheltenham Ladies' College, where I learned the meaning of "mufti" (no school uniform) and of the "baths" (swimming pool). While there I had to go down to the University of London to write a Junior Matriculation exam in English composition on the same day as students in Canada would be writing it. Even had I known the questions beforehand, this would not have helped, as the examination consisted of writing an essay on one of a choice of subjects. I can hardly credit it now, but I was allowed to go alone over a hundred miles away on the bus to a small hotel in London, to find a restaurant for supper, and then go to the opera at Covent Garden, where I saw *The Flying Dutchman* from the highest row in the theatre. I gloried in my independence without a moment of fear. Today I marvel at how carefree life used to be.

Next morning I managed to get myself to the right classroom where I chose to write my essay on the quotation, "One hour of glorious life is worth an age without a name." To illustrate this sentiment, I described my experience of watching the coronation procession in all its splendour and what a thrilling event it had been for me. When I returned to Canada I found that I had indeed passed the exam, and for at least one full year after that adventure, I was a fervent royalist.

A different sort of experience in London had more lasting consequences. During the winter before my trip, an Anglican minister had come to our school in Toronto where he preached a moving sermon that ignited my adolescent interest in becoming a missionary in Africa to convert the "heathen". I looked him up and had an enjoyable tea with him and his wife, and he accompanied me from his home in a taxi, where, to my shock and horror, he groped me. From then on I lost all interest in pursuing religious causes or careers. It was many years before I became aware that there might have been a link between my adolescent religious fervour and my awakening sexuality.

The third major event was far more devastating. In November of that same year of 1937, I was awakened one Sunday night by loud groans coming from my father's bedroom. My heart racing, I went to see what was the matter, and was terrified to see him suffering from an extreme pain that had gripped him. I had never known him to be sick before. No home remedies were effective, and at morning light my mother summoned an ambulance to take her and my father to the hospital. Later I learned that he had required an operation for an intestinal blockage caused by adhesions from an appendectomy he had undergone many years before. The operation was successful, and for several days we rejoiced. Then an infection set in and the picture became graver. Those were the days before antibiotics, and the only treatment was another operation.

I remember playing outside on that warm November day and waiting for my mother's return from the hospital. As I saw her coming around the corner I knew, before she said a word, from her stooped posture and slowed movements, that my father had died. My first words were, "Don't worry, Mother. We'll look after you." I think the die was cast that day that I would make looking after people in trouble my life's profession. I was not aware then of my own immense loss, grief, or need, a denial that became cemented into my character.

We three children were all sent to relatives or friends until the funeral. I went to Cousin Mary Leacock in Aurora, Stephen Leacock's sister-in-law. She lived on a farm property thirty miles out of Toronto where we used to go for day visits once or twice a year. I felt a little as if I had been banished, although I did not want to face what was happening at home. As I was being tucked into bed that first night, Cousin Mary said, in what I assume was an effort to normalize the situation, "It's so hard to get one's arms out of the way when you are lying on your side and trying to sleep. Wouldn't it be nice to be able to take them off and put them on the floor until morning?" The image this conveyed must have fed into all the fantasies of mutilation and injury I was having at the time because of what had happened to my father. It has remained a potent image even after all these years and has not been relegated to the scrap heap of memories like so many others.

When we children returned home to prepare for the funeral,

we found it frightening. Dad was laid out in an open coffin in our living room, surrounded by wreaths and flowers for the customary three days before the hearse came to take him to the funeral at the church and burial at the cemetery. I was terrified by this made-up dead body that no longer seemed like my father, and which transformed our home into a scary place.

After the excitement and activity were over and the out-of-town relatives went home to resume their lives, Mother collapsed in her grief. Without her husband, she was lost. She shut herself in her room and was incapable of comforting us children. I remember knocking on her bedroom door and begging her to come out to eat. I was frightened by her behaviour and felt her absence keenly, even though she was physically present. I interpreted her isolation as rejection and questioned whether she could love me if she was unwilling to listen to our pleas to come out even when we had prepared something special for her Sunday meal. Her depression seemed to last for months. She remained withdrawn, unwilling even to play the piano, although occasionally she would brighten when we asked her to play something we liked, such as "In a Monastery Garden". Before her marriage she had graduated from the Royal Conservatory of Music. She had been a piano teacher and played the organ in a downtown church on Sundays, but she had given that up to raise her family. I remember her telling us that when she was a young girl, she had cut her long hair and sold the switch to pay for music lessons.

Now she was facing financial problems again, with sparse knowledge about such things. Like many women of her generation, she had relied on my father to handle all the business and money matters, and, of course, he had no idea that he would die suddenly at forty-nine, so nothing was arranged. Fortunately, his law firm took over handling the estate. In addition to these practical concerns, Mother felt that all their friends had been couples now had little use for a widow in their social life. My father had three unmarried sisters who doted on him, but they only tolerated her.

The oldest aunt was Janet, or Nana, who was twenty years older than my father. She was more of a mother to him than his actual mother and advised him and guided his decisions as he grew up. Letters indicate a deep affection between them. Nana went to the University of Toronto and got a degree in French Literature. She must have been one of the very early women in this program and I remember her telling us how she had been made to leave the class and wait in the hall when the professor was reading or talking about a racy modern poet, such as Rimbaud or Baudelaire. She had a long career teaching high school students at Galt Collegiate, now called Cambridge. I remember sharing the family pride when she received a decoration from King George V for her outstanding contribution to the field of education.

Nana lived with her sister, Aunt Allie, who kept house for her and never worked outside the family because she had suffered from poliomyelitis as a child and was left with a lame leg and a brace. We frequently drove up to visit them on a Sunday and one of my memories is of a large china chicken that sat on a table in the dining room. We would rush to lift the lid to see if there was a newly "laid" egg inside. There always was, much to my delight.

Auntie May, the third sister, lived in New York where she had trained as a nurse and obtained the job as nurse-companion and friend to the wealthy widow of a lumber tycoon who owned a house on 68th Street, a country estate on Long Island, and an Adirondack cottage. May was the toughest and I was always frightened of her because of her sharp, cutting, often angry tongue. I thought her strange because of her unusual clothing. She often wore a suit with breeches, a matching jacket, shirt and tie. My sister Mary was cosseted by the aunts, taken to England or for summers in Long Island, and was the object of expensive birthday and Christmas gifts. Their involvement with Mary certainly put her further out of my orbit and their physical and psychological distance from Mother meant they were not too much help to her in her distress, but Auntie May did nonetheless pay my monthly fifteen-dollar allowance for several years after Dad died.

Mother often used to say that she wished we were like a Chinese family with many generations living together. We were grateful that we had school on weekdays and could escape the heavy gloom of the house. Gradually, after months had passed, the atmosphere lightened and I began to feel that there was another side to my mother. She made a few new friends, often widows like herself. She developed an interest in the C.C.F., the social democratic Co-operative Commonwealth Federation party that was to become today's New Democratic Party. She was much impressed by a biography of Jennie Lee, the British Labour Party politician, and this perhaps led her to examine the idea of a more independent role for women. Another new interest was the Christian Science Church, where one of her friends was a committed member. Somehow she was convinced that she could combine its beliefs with the care she was still receiving from medical practitioners, saying that Christian Science was like a market where you could take what you needed and leave the rest aside—a convenient view indeed. Despite these new interests in her life, however, she rarely seemed to me to be a happy person again. I used to feel that I wanted to flee just when she needed me most.

I began to have a more mature understanding of my mother a few years later when I did a formal interview with her for a sociology assignment on different family patterns. For the first time I learned some details of her own childhood, and that the lack of intimacy in our mother-daughter relationship had been her lot as well. Throughout her childhood, her mother had been ill, spending many of her days in bed, with the household required to be very quiet so she should not be disturbed.

By the time I was in university my boyfriend (who would later be my first husband) lived in a room nearby without kitchen privileges. He used to illegally keep a few food items in a suitcase under his bed. In 1941, obviously trying to kill two birds with one stone, I proposed that my mother make dinners for him for a small fee. His company did wonders for her mood—in fact, for that of the whole household. It was like a miracle to hear her laugh again. Later, when I was married and living in Kingston, she agreed to bicycle sixty miles with us to visit a friend at Smith's Falls, and it seemed that she was becoming a more complete, fulfilled person than she had ever been during her marriage and widowhood. Her interests were wider and she was less bound by "shoulds" and "oughts".

Before the end of the year after my father's death, we had to sell the house on Lawrence Crescent and move into a rented duplex. This meant sharing a room with my sister, something I disliked intensely. If she found I had left any of my clothes not hung up, she threw them all on the floor. I imagine she found sharing space with me equally unpleasant, since up to that time we had always been able to have our own space.

Eventually we were able to work out some kind of peaceful co-existence, largely by ignoring one another. And, of course, we had good times together as well. I admired her style, her popularity, and her achievements, and I would have given my eye teeth for her extra three or four inches of height. Not too long after, she married and moved away.

Throughout our lives, however, my identifying label would be that of "Mary's sister". As the only child in the family for five years, she had become the favoured one. It was not surprising that our relationship was problematic; the aunts would give her a large or expensive gift at Christmas, when I received a box of initialled handkerchiefs from them. I was told that I must do as well as she had at Havergal and, while our father was still alive, I felt I had to compete with her for his attention.

My brother John, as the youngest member of the family, was close enough in age so that we sometimes played together, but once we were in school we seemed to go our separate ways. He had a stutter as a child, and when young he was made to read aloud from the Bible after we came home from church on Sundays. I found his agony in bringing out the words painful to witness, and did not feel this humiliation could possibly be a cure. These sessions lasted until my father's death. Like many boys, he had a turbulent adolescence, and there were several changes of school as a result of his misdemeanors. As we grew into adulthood our tastes became more alike and we became the friends neither of us was with our sister Mary. He was unwaveringly supportive of me later when my first marriage came apart and I so badly needed supporters. I was proud of his success as a marine biologist, and of his efforts to obtain a PhD, a feat achieved in his mid-thirties. I regretted he could not seem to live without the periodic alcoholic blowouts that inevitably made his life difficult. He was an extremely intelligent, very loveable man who died much too young at age 62.

Joan's grandfather, Alexander Carter, with her father,
Fredric Charteris Carter, c. 1921.

CHAPTER TWO

The Roberts of Frederiction

GOODRIDGE ROBERTS WAS BORN in 1904 into one of Canada's most celebrated literary families. His father, Theodore, was a prolific writer of tremendous energy and self-discipline. As well as short stories and poems, he had published thirty-five novels and over one hundred periodical pieces by 1914 in addition to his work as a literary editor and newspaper columnist. Supporting the family with his writings was difficult and perhaps explained what seemed to be a great restlessness. When his first child Goodridge was born in 1904, it was not in the family home province of New Brunswick but in Barbados where his parents lived for two years after their marriage. Throughout Goodridge's childhood and adolescence, his family was constantly on the move. They lived in countless different houses and locations in Canada, England, and France, and Goodridge attended many different schools before finishing high school. At one point his father tried farming. The children went to school in a horse and buggy but at the end of one school year the farm was abandoned because it was not financially viable.

Sir Charles G. D. Roberts, Goodridge's uncle, highly popular for his animal stories, was the first Canadian to be knighted for poetry. Charles' cousin Bliss Carman, sometimes called the "unofficial poet laureate of Canada" was even better known. Roberts and Carman, together with Duncan Campbell Scott and Archibald Lampman, are known as the "Confederation Poets", credited with being the first to write with a distinctively Canadian voice in English. Their work had a marked effect on the development of poetry in the years leading up to the World War I.

Uncle Charles was noted among family and friends for having a raffish air. On one occasion he answered the doorbell when Goodridge rang with a vacuum cord in one hand, completely nude. Charles was very interested in Goodridge's promising, potential contribution to the "clan", as he called them, before he died in 1943.

Bliss Carman may have been the most talented member of that generation. He was certainly the most renowned. But as he spent most of his adult life in the United States after his university days at Edinburgh, Fredericton, and Harvard, and died when Goodridge was twenty-five, Goodridge never got to know him well.

Goodridge was the only boy born to Theodore and his wife, Frances Seymour Allen. A sister died as a young child and the only memory of her that Goodridge retained was of her being propped up after death for a photograph because his parents did not have one. It seemed ghoulish to him. Dorothy, a couple of years his junior, wrote poetry as a child and had a chapbook published at the age of fourteen. It is possible that Goodridge might have chosen to become a writer had Dorothy not already assumed the mantle. His love of poetry was profound and in his adult life, teaching English was always the only other occupation he could imagine himself being capable of performing. Dorothy married August Leisner and they spent many years at State College, Pennsylvania where they were both professors. Dorothy continued to write and publish throughout her life. Theodora, or Teddy as she was called, was the youngest and Goodridge's favourite. To my knowledge she never wrote and after marriage seemed to have inherited some of her father's restlessness. She bought houses one after another, fixed them up, sold them, and moved on to another more suitable one, only to repeat the pattern.

I never met Goodridge's father since he died only a few months after we came together. He did not seem to figure prominently in

Goodridge's mother with Goodridge and sister Dorothy, c. 1909.

[top]Goodridge as a boy scout in England, c. 1915.
[bottom] Summer 1929, Nashwaak River, N.B.
Goodridge Roberts standing and painting (left), Charles G.D. Roberts standing (right), Edith Roberts (Charles' daughter) kneeling, Frances Roberts (Goodridge's mother) preparing meal, Theodora (Goodridge's younger sister) bare-legged.

Goodridge's adult life, though he spoke cordially about him as he did about all his older relatives. As the embodiment of "father figure" Theodore may have had to share the territory in Goodridge's psyche with both Max Stern, owner of the Dominion Gallery, who provided economic sustenance, and then Dr. Miguel Prados, who provided psychological support. There were many other family members who sustained and supported Goodridge. It was his mother's brother, Tom, who put a painting of Goodridge's in the Moncton County Fair where it won first prize of five dollars. It was his aunt Ada Allen, one of his mother's sisters and a teacher at the High School of Montreal who gave him room and board while he was at the École des Beaux Arts, and his aunt Mary Fanton Roberts on his father's side, editor of the magazine *Arts and Decoration* in New York, who was instrumental in getting him enrolled in the Arts Students League in New York and who introduced him to her artistic friends and contacts such as Isadora Duncan and Theodore Dreiser.

I met Goodridge's mother when she came to visit us twice in Montreal in the early 1960s. I remember her as a rather proper, reserved but kindly woman. When she died in 1966 and the news came by telephone, our son Tim was four years old and proclaimed through his tears that he *needed* a grandmother. This spoke to her good-heartedness, but Goodridge was not able to feel close to her and there were lasting resentments. Their relationship was quite amicable if somewhat distant. He told me of his childhood memory of feeling her jealousy of his affection for his Caribbean nursemaid who returned to Fredericton with the family after his birth in Barbados. In his late twenties, his mother had refused his request to bring his friend, the painter Ernst Neumann, to visit because he was Jewish. He was also very hurt by her having thrown out hundreds of drawings that he had done while a student in New York in the 1920s.

There were no painters in his family, but this is what Goodridge wanted to be from the time he was about ten years old, and the environment in which he grew up certainly encouraged appreciation of the arts. After returning to Fredericton from Barbados, in another few years they would leave for two years in England (1909-11) and then again for four years while his father was in the army during World War I. He recalled childhood visits to Kensington Gardens and a certain quality of the light as having stimulated and reinforced his interest in becoming a painter. He was only four when his mother took him to his first art exhibition, Roger Fry's *Manet and the Post-Impressionists*, at London's Grafton Gallery.

After finishing high school in Fredericton he began his art education when he was nineteen at the École des Beaux Arts in Montreal. There was strong emphasis on working from plaster casts and in the first year he won medals for drawing, decorative painting, and ornamental modelling. In the second year he was less diligent and won none, having decided that "art was not to be come by in this way," and he spent more time reading poetry and sketching outside the classroom. His Beaux Arts years instilled in him the enormous self-discipline he would show during his entire career.

He went to New York in 1926 and spent nearly two years at the Arts Students League where he was exposed for the first time to the works of Cézanne, Matisse, and Picasso, as well as Giotto, Goya, and Velasquez. His teachers taught him to see the significant aspects of art, linking the art of the past to the art of the present. It was in New York that his basic approach to painting was formed, as he studied under John Sloan, Max Weber, and Boardman Robinson.

He returned to Canada in 1928. He worked at first near Fredericton and then around Ottawa and the Gatineau when his parents moved there. By this time it was the Great Depression and difficult to survive on the $1.50 a week he earned from teaching painting to two pupils. Two stories survive from those days in the early '30s. Françoise Sagan, the French novelist, had a sister, Madeleine Quoirez, who was studying under Goodridge. To his amazement she became enamoured of him without any encouragement beyond his customary politeness. She was returning to France and said that if he would not accompany her she would throw herself off the ship. He thought this was just hysterical exaggeration until he learned that in fact she had done so.

The second story was equally horrifying. It concerned a chap he knew who was very ill. A direct transfusion was considered essential. Goodridge volunteered, but as he lay on the gurney, beside another one on which lay the patient, the man became paler and paler and finally died. It was before the days of blood typing and they were likely incompatible.

In 1933, Queen's University in Kingston provided Goodridge with a temporary way out of his financial worries. He was appointed Resident Artist for three years, funded by a grant from the Carnegie Foundation, and was able to marry Marian Willson in December 1933. His responsibilities at Queen's were to teach drawing and painting to both Queen's students and members of the public, as well as organize conferences and workshops. Unfortunately, little time remained to concentrate on his own work. Back in Montreal in 1936, he started a private art school with Ernst Neumann, resumed painting, and, by 1938, had amassed enough good work to start exhibiting. He used to say that he had had thirty exhibitions before purchases covered more than the costs. He lived and painted in Québec until he went overseas as an Official War Artist during World War II. After leaving the Air Force he continued to live in Montreal, painting figures and still life in the winter and in the summer seeking out spots in the Laurentians, the Eastern Townships, and the Lower St. Lawrence where the landscape appealed to him. It was during this period that his marriage to Marian ended in divorce. Our life together began six years later.

CHAPTER THREE

Ottawa

ON SEPTEMBER 3, 1939, a day before I turned seventeen, World War II was declared. Like many young women at the time, I thought of becoming a nurse, but my stern Auntie May, herself a nurse, scotched that idea and said firmly that I was to go to university. It was difficult for me to decide what program to follow because I had taken no science courses at Havergal College and this limited my options. The extra courses I had taken—Greek, to the Junior Matriculation level, Latin, to the Senior Matriculation level, French, and German—might have led me to specialize in languages, but this did not have sufficient appeal to me.

As a teenager I had wondered what I would do later, and told my father that I had thought of going into law at university. He rejected such an idea, telling me that it was not a field for women. If that is the case, I replied, because I love sports so much, I will become a physical education teacher. His response to that suggestion was, "And what will happen to your brains?" Those were powerful messages, clearly indicating problems for women in getting higher education. Finally I chose a new four-year honours program at the University of Toronto called "Social and Philosophical Studies", in which a variety of humanities and social sciences could be taken in first year, followed by specialization in one social science during the three subsequent years. I chose sociology. It was quite new at the University of Toronto, and there were only about fifteen students in our class. We became a close-knit, intimate group, even though we came from different backgrounds. The many new ideas I was exposed to during my four years in university had a profound effect on me at that time and into the future. It gave me the beginning of an intellectual framework, which helped me examine and reject many of the social and political beliefs that were current in the middle class of the day.

Perhaps one of the most significant factors in this was my friendship with the Coleman family. Kay, a fellow student in sociology, became my closest friend and has remained so. Her father, a country surgeon who had moved to Toronto, took out my appendix at the Salvation Army Grace Hospital when classes were over. Kay often brought me to her home for lunch where her mother made the most delicious tea biscuits and her father had his medical office. If anyone mentioned a symptom, particularly his wife, he would say in his gruff but kindly manner, "See me in my office." Kay was the youngest child; her two brothers were out of the house, but her social worker sister Helen, who was at the time in the Women's Air Force, had a great deal of influence on Kay and thus indirectly on me. Her occupation as a social worker and her rather dogmatic left-wing political views, as well as the exciting books I was reading for classes, opened a whole new, vibrant, and engaging world to me. Before I knew it I was doing door-to-door canvassing for the by-election of a C.C.F. social democrat and sounding as if I knew what life and politics was all about. I also learned how different family life could be, not only with warmth and caring, but also with all members still living. My friendship with Kay was cemented that summer when we got a job from my cousin to paint a large wooden cottage on Lake Couchiching near Orillia. In deference to my recent abdominal operation, Kay offered to do the all high ladder work.

The economics, biology, psychology, political science, and anthropology courses continued to capture my interest and they seemed to have relevance in my life. Our anthropology prof forbade us to knit in class, so we countered by secretly knitting his pregnant wife a huge layette, knowing he would be shamed into withdrawing his prohibition, and that proved to be accurate. I thrived academically and was able to thwart the fellow student known for having a photographic memory, whatever that might portend, and win the modest B. Sadowski Award for highest marks in my second and third year.

When I was seventeen, I met the man who would become my first husband. We were both working at the same summer resort hotel in Muskoka, where his father was chef. I started out as a kitchen helper, then became a waitress. Vincent Thomas was Welsh, a few years older than I, handsome, intelligent, and musical, with artistic ambitions but no formal schooling beyond tenth grade. He could tell wonderful and often hilarious stories, especially about his early years in Wales. He was a charmer, and he definitely charmed me. I was impressed by his untutored artistic talent. Every night, as our relationship progressed, he would leave at my work station a delightful little ink drawing he had done on a three-by-five-inch index card. Susceptible as I was to this type of sweet seduction, I soon began to spend most of my free time with him.

Summer relationships allowed for all kinds of difference in background, but it was taken as a given that they were temporary and would not continue into the winter. Soon we would return to our normal lives, I would go back to university, and Vincent would go to whatever kind of unskilled job he could find. He challenged me by saying with great conviction that he knew I would not want to have anything to do with him once I left the resort. I protested that this was untrue and that my affection was not that fickle, false, or flighty.

That affirmation was to have major consequences. When, after the summer, I continued to go out with Vincent, I was turning away from the narrow-minded, bourgeois, class-conscious Toronto in which I had always lived, and once I had violated its taboos, there was no turning back. Even our marriage did not restore my former status. I had succumbed to my sister's advice to join a sorority lest I be isolated and unhappy, but I suffered worse problems in trying to integrate Vincent into my social life. Social class was unimportant with my fellow sociology students who came from many walks of life, but that was not so in the sorority world.

A powerful influence on changing social attitudes, however, was the War. By the early 1940s people in Canada were feeling mounting fear and anxiety as the news worsened. The mood in Toronto at that time was intensely sombre and patriotic. In 1942 Vincent enlisted in the army without telling me beforehand. He was soon gone for his basic training in the Royal Canadian Ordnance Corps. Even though this seemed somewhat safer than the infantry, I was still devastated, certain that he would be killed. In early 1943, while he was stationed outside Kingston and facing duty overseas, we decided to marry. I am not sure what motivated us, but with the world drama unfolding as it did, there was a feeling of inevitability about it. I rationalized our decision by saying that it would be better to be a war widow than never to have been married. Also, Kay had married Ed Percival the previous year after meeting and taking him to a Sadie Hawkins dance. My mother was less than pleased with our plan even though I was now twenty and had known Vincent for nearly three years. "What if you get pregnant?" she asked, principally because she feared that I would end up as a single mother without any means of support, though this was never made explicit. Her preoccupation with our future was behind one of her many references to her will. Mary's husband Bill, now a doctor, was serving in the medical corps in Italy. Mother suggested on one occasion that perhaps she should not split her estate into equal thirds because Bill's earning power after the war was over would be infinitely greater than Vincent's. This brought a flood of tears from Mary and her offended response that Bill might not get back alive.

Like many other wartime marriages, our wedding could not have been simpler. It took place on a weekend evening in Kingston, performed by a Justice of the Peace without guests and in the presence of two witnesses, one of them the wife of the Justice in her bedroom slippers. A honeymoon was out of the question. Vincent had to return to the base on Monday morning, and I took the train back to Toronto for four final months of university classes. With classes over I moved to Kingston to be near Vincent whenever he was off duty. Somehow I learned of a little two-room cottage on the shore of Lake Ontario, close to Wolfe Island and adjacent to the Barriefield army base. In fact, the obstacle course for training recruits was right behind the dwelling. We bought the cottage for $50, lived there for six months, and were able to sell it for $75.

As I now see it, it was mostly fun, playing house. We had to carry our water from a spring about a hundred yards away and we only had our bicycles for the transport of groceries from Kingston, about three or four kilometres away. When the weather grew cold, we wheeled hundred-pound (45 kg) sacks of coal home for our little stove. Our neighbor was Grant MacDonald, an artist. He was often joined by his friend Herbert Whittaker, the eminent Toronto theatre critic. One day we were informed that a number of German prisoners-of-war had escaped from nearby Fort Henry. We were assured that they would be quickly rounded up but meanwhile precautions were encouraged and on no account should help or food be given or confrontations be undertaken. That first night was more than a little frightening—doors were locked and axes at the ready under the bed. One by one they were all recaptured and no civilians were harmed.

The war did not help couples beginning married life. Prior to embarkation, Vincent was transferred to Nova Scotia, and I obtained a government job in Ottawa at the Department of Labour. When Vincent obtained a short embarkation leave we were able to spend a few days together cross-country skiing in the Gatineau Hills outside Ottawa. I was not to see him again for two years. During that time, each of us would experience events that would change us greatly, and that we could share only in letters. As Vincent was in active combat in Holland, many of his experiences were traumatic, and

Vincent on leave before embarking to England, 1944.

[top] Joan and Vincent, c. 1942.
[bottom] Joan with axe to open waterhole in the winter of 1949-50.

even though my fears that he would be killed or wounded proved groundless, by the time he came home his carefree, youthful innocence was gone. The horrors of war and the death of comrades had inexorably left their mark.

January 1944 saw me in my first real job and Vincent in various army camps preparing to go overseas in April. I was rooming in the Ottawa apartment of a woman with a young baby whose husband was in England with the R.C.A.F. I got breakfast there, but ate all my dinners at Murray's in the Lord Elgin Hotel before heading home to my solitary room. The first happy flush I felt at having a job in Ottawa wore off after a few months, and even the handsome salary of $2,160 a year, that included a cost-of-living bonus, was not enough to counteract the growing boredom and loneliness I felt. I was in the Labour Legislation Branch, and my job involved writing up changes in labour regulations that would be incorporated into legislation. They were then published in *The Labour Gazette*, an excruciatingly boring publication issued monthly. Thus, if there were changes in safety provisions for boilermakers, for example, I would go back to the legislation under which boilermakers operated, determine what effect the new rules would have, and then record it in understandable English. Everything I wrote had to be gone over with a fine tooth comb, and it was usually returned to me covered with red pencil marks and instructions for a rewrite.

My boss, Margaret Macintosh, was one of three women who shared a house in Rockcliffe and who, despite being women, exercised power in wartime Ottawa. Another of the housemates was Charlotte Whitton, who later became the controversial mayor of Ottawa. The third was responsible for introducing unemployment insurance in Canada.

The dullness of the work was made worse by the atmosphere in the office, which was oppressive and gloomy. The staff consisted of one man and five women, two of them elderly, the juice quite squeezed out of them as they wound up lifetime careers in the civil service. Two of the younger women were brainy idealists who soon took off to do research for the Ontario C.C.F. (now the New Democratic Party).

Life for me was made bearable by the presence in Ottawa of my friends Kay Coleman-Percival and her husband Ed. Kay has remained my close friend over the past seventy years. They suggested that we sublet an apartment together for the summer months. Before long, we found a suitable place in Ottawa south, an upper flat on Wilton Crescent, overlooking a large pond. It belonged to Sergeant Popki of the R.C.M.P., who was going off on a training course. He may or may not have been with the anti-subversive squad, but, as long-term dissenters we enjoyed the minor *frisson* of renting his flat.

The summer was idyllic. On one of the hot days, and there were many, the government would close offices at 3 p.m. (air-conditioning had not yet been introduced). We would rush home, change our clothes and head for the tennis club on our bicycles. Being young, the heat didn't bother us. The club was right on the Rideau River and in those far-off days it was unpolluted. After our tennis game we would jump in for a cooling swim. We were young and the world was our oyster.

I had to decide what to do with my annual holidays, the last part of August. Kay and Ed had plans, so I had to arrange something on my own. Fortunately, I heard about a two-week adult education program called Camp Macdonald (later Laquemac), sponsored jointly by Macdonald College's Adult Education Program and Laval University's Social Science Faculty, at that time under the progressive direction of the renowned Dominican, Père Georges-Henri Lévesque. It was a bilingual program aimed at training group leaders and professionals from rural and urban organizations. Happily, I decided to register. The experience proved to be very important for me. I found the program exciting, immensely stimulating, and years ahead of its time. I returned the next summer in 1945 with Kay after helping to design the program with the Laval group in Québec City. My

French improved so much that planning weekend that I actually dreamt in French. Some of the Francophones attending later went on to Ottawa to work in the bureaucracy during the Trudeau years. The camp functioned extremely well in the two languages and there was a real spirit of wanting to embrace the other's culture.

Several Americans were also at the camp. One was Zylphia Horton, from the Highlander Folk School in Tennessee; and another was Lois Timmins, at that time a collector of French-Canadian folk songs. There were also participants from the co-op movement, from urban organizations, and from the press and radio, as well as some unattached professionals. The daytime workshops focused on techniques of working with groups. At night we sat around campfires for singsongs in both languages (I have never forgotten "Youpee, youpee, sur la rivière ..."). The location was beautiful, in the Eastern Townships on the shores of Lake Memphramagog at what was usually a girls' camp. This setting contributed an appropriate inspiration for the idealism that prevailed. As we talked and talked, the One World we hoped for as the end of the war approached or, at the very least, a harmonious Québec, seemed attainable.

It was heady stuff. I returned to Ottawa full of the enthusiasm and optimism of youth, to a job that seemed more useless than ever. There seemed few options, since the route from a degree in sociology to appropriate employment was not clearly evident in those early days of the discipline in Canada. After graduation I had first naively tried the maximum security federal prison in Kingston. I suspect that the warden hid his amusement at my request for a job there, although he graciously talked to me in his office for a considerable period of time. I also offered my services to the local newspaper, the *Kingston Whig Standard*, with equal lack of success.

At the University of Toronto, the Bloor Street building housing the Sociology Department also contained the School of Social Work. The chair of our department used to threaten us with "ending up down the hall" if we didn't work harder, so we absorbed the notion that social work was for the less intelligent. Counteracting that prejudice was the knowledge that Kay's sister had been a social worker for many years and was clearly intelligent.

As my Ottawa job paled more and more, a career in social work began to seem an increasingly viable alternative. At Laquemac I had met a couple of social workers from Montreal with avant-garde opinions, so I decided to look into the graduate program in Social Work at McGill University. Because of the War, they were offering a continuous eighteen-month program instead of the normal two-year program, on the assumption that social workers would soon be badly needed. My goal was to acquire qualifications that would enable me to get a job when Vincent came home. The added attraction was that the master's degree would let me find work anywhere in Canada, and the return of the armed forces at the end of the war would open up jobs in my field. I was conscious of the fact that if Vincent survived the war, he did not have any career credentials. One concern, however, was that leaving my first permanent position to go back to school meant that it would be five or more years before my salary would equal that of the job I was leaving and I might have to continue for some time managing on the $66 a month paid to a soldier's wife.

Ed was being posted to Petawawa and would later go overseas, so both Kay and I applied to the Montreal School of Social Work, soon to affiliate with McGill University. We were interviewed at the Chateau Laurier by the director, Dorothy King. We were both accepted on the spot and I was awarded the bursary I was seeking to cover my fees.

I resigned from my government job and we packed all our belongings into Kay and Ed's ancient Chevrolet and headed for Montreal, a city neither of us knew. My only visit to the city had been in 1937 en route to England, but some of the Montrealers I had met at Laquemac had given me a favourable view of the city. The fact that it was not in Toronto may have led us to believe that a university in Montreal would have higher intellectual standards than "the school down the hall", although some uncertainty must have persisted, since we also registered in a McGill graduate seminar in sociology during our first term, in case the program in social work proved to offer insufficient mental challenge. I have to admit we were horrible intellectual snobs.

CHAPTER FOUR

A Professional Career

GIVEN OUR FIRST EXPERIENCE in Montreal, it was just as well that Kay and I were predisposed to view it positively. We drove along Dorchester (now René Lévesque) Boulevard looking for a place to spend the night, and ended up at a large, rather rundown rooming-house, the Bell Lodge, near Crescent Street, that was cheap and had a huge backyard for parking. The next morning we found our car had been broken into and our winter coats were stolen. Mine was a Harris tweed, practically new, that I had saved up to purchase and loved dearly. We phoned the police immediately. Today such a call would probably prove futile, but at that time it produced a detective in a car who, after taking down our story, proceeded to take us on a tour of the seedy pawnshops on Craig Street in search of the missing coats. Pawnshops have always seemed bleak, melancholy places to me, filled as they are with mementos of lost hopes and failed accomplishments. Our search went on for a couple of days and finally the coats were located. For us, the reward (in addition to the coats) was the experience of exploring the seamier parts of Montreal and being able to entertain our fellow students and staff with the story, surely a huge advantage for would-be social workers.

Our first home was a small, third-floor room on Côte-des-Neiges just above Sherbrooke Street, where a large apartment building stands today. It was in a very large Victorian house that had been turned into a rooming house. Our room cost us each $12.50 a month.

Joan and friend Kay Percival's "first home" —a small room at
3441 Côte-des-Neiges, Montreal, 1944.

There was only one bed, and a very uncomfortable chair that could be unfolded every night to provide another sleeping space. We took turns in the bed, one week off and one on. The tenants were a varied group. On our floor there was one bathroom and a large room shared by three young girls who worked in offices. We used to exchange casual remarks with them, and once we asked one of them if she would like to come out with us that evening. She replied that she thought she would just stay in and "rest her nails". There were two elderly sisters, the Misses Carruthers, memorable for saying "What a relief" on all sorts of occasions. Because he behaved so furtively, we were convinced a youngish man with a thick accent calling himself a Swede was a German spy. When we didn't have all the facts, we invented recklessly.

On occasional weekends we drove to Toronto on old Highway 2 to visit our families. It was a risky undertaking, often including long stops at a garage for repairs. We had so many flat tires that it became a challenge and we were soon able to change a tire in twelve minutes.

In the winter we began skiing. Sometimes we would take the streetcar up the hill to Mount Royal, and there was so little traffic we could then ski right down Côte-des-Neiges to our rooming-house. On weekends we would take the Petit Train du Nord to the Laurentians, ski down to a lower village on the Maple Leaf Trail, and pick up the train heading home. Climbing the mountain was part of the fun in those days. There were only rope tows and we considered using them beneath our dignity. The train was always raucous with song and laughter on the way home, and it was great fun despite our fatigue and sore muscles.

One Saturday night we decided to stay in the Laurentians over-night at whatever we could find. We knocked at the door of a farmhouse in Saint-Sauveur, and the francophone family there agreed to give us supper and a bed for a moderate fee. As we sat in the living room we began to talk about the war. It was all the fault of the Jews, they said, showing us newspapers containing items about the *Protocols of the Elders of Zion*, and describing Jews in horrifyingly anti-Semitic language. We did our best to disabuse them of their beliefs, but our French was limited, so we gave up and decided that the best thing to do was to go to bed.

This was not the Québec we had experienced at Laquemac. This was the Québec of Duplessis, Adrien Arcand (the fascist, demagogic journalist who founded and led several extremely right-wing, anti-Semitic political parties), the Padlock Law, the persecution of Jehovah's Witnesses, quotas for Jews at McGill, and the exclusion of Jews in Laurentian hotels. Our overnight experience indicates how widespread such sentiments were sixty years ago. It was in marked contrast to our winter weekend at Laval University.

Meanwhile, we attended our classes at McGill. They were located in a grand old house at 3600 University Street, full of beautiful wood panelling and other vestiges of more elegant days. There were only about twelve of us in the accelerated program, so the atmosphere was very informal. We had some fine teachers: Frank Scott, poet and constitutional lawyer, one of the founders of the C.C.F., for our studies on social policy, and Dr. Miguel Prados, psychoanalyst, for a few lectures on psychopathology, to mention only two.

My supervisor in the second half of the course, Celia Deschin, a tiny but feisty woman on leave from Adelphi University in New York, had a great influence on me and in fact was a breath of fresh air to the whole Montreal social work community because of the conferences and symposia she gave here. She became a sort of guru and friend to Kay and me and we took her one weekend on a camping trip to the Laurentians where she woke up in a tent beside the highway with a cow mooing at the entrance. For a Brooklyn resident it was the equivalent of a lion on an African safari. Her husband, a *New York Times* photographer, took nude photos of each of us to send to our husbands overseas, supposedly to make our absence easier to bear, but in any case much appreciated.

In the spring of 1945 Kay and I were asked to join a group

establishing a housing co-op on Lorne Crescent, a once elegant residential street east of the university. The house was owned by Dr. Raymond Boyer, a chemistry professor at McGill and a committed communist. We had found the English-speaking community to be divided into the Protestant old-timers, some of whom were the wealthy power brokers of the city and quite conservative in outlook, and another large group of artists and intellectuals, often Jewish, who were left-wing, sometimes communist, but with different social views and values and very conscious of what was happening in Europe and in the war. This group provided a sort of alternative community, not only of ideas and moral support but also of access to services and facilities unacceptable in the larger Québec society of the day. For example, through word of mouth one could find doctors who performed abortions, who provided fertility treatment, who helped with end-of-life care and the like. It was the same for other professions. This was the society that Kay and I identified with.

We moved gratefully from our cramped quarters in the rooming -house to Boyer's large Victorian dwelling at the end of the crescent and soon found ourselves among a group of people whose ideas and conversations were wonderfully invigorating. We were ten young people, including three married couples, professionals and students, several from minority groups. In addition to Kay and me, our group included Sylvia and Glenn Warner. He was an engineer who had lost an arm as a result of a sarcoma he developed at the Chalk River nuclear facility. Eddie and Marian de Jean were both notable educators. Eddie would go on to receive the O.B.E. for his work in the schools of Bermuda. I recall little about Ruth and Clayton Gray except that Clayton was a historian, writer, and freelance journalist. Freda Wales was studying physical education at McGill, and Frances Cohen, sister-in-law of Raymond Boyer, felt that she had special status because of this and tried to impose rules on us about our usage of the house, but we waited for one of our interminable Sunday meetings before accepting any decisions. On one memorable occasion Paul Robeson, in Montreal for a concert, came to visit and sang for us. We were all overwhelmed by his wonderful baritone voice which filled the living room.

We were unaware that Dr. Boyer would be implicated in the spy hunt following the defection to Canadian authorities of Igor Gouzenko from the Russian Embassy in July of 1945. Gouzenko left with secret documents implicating a number of Canadians in passing scientific secrets to the Russians. We agreed with many others that the Russians had been our allies throughout the war and that scientific knowledge should be shared with them. There was a considerable time lapse, but finally Boyer's arrest, and that of a number of others, took place when we were out of the city visiting friends in the Laurentians. We were spared the R.C.M.P.'s early morning efforts in February 1946 to find Boyer at the house; he had not actually lived there since our co-op started. The R.C.M.P. found some telephone numbers on the wall by the telephone table and copied them down diligently, but they must have been chagrined to discover that the numbers had been recorded by our cook when she was looking for a company that could supply her brand of corset. That was one of the few light moments during the period when the Gouzenko Affair, as it was called, cast a severe pall over left-wing sympathizers in Montreal. When it was finally all over, nine of the twenty arrested had been acquitted. Boyer received two years in prison and Gordon Lunan had his sentence extended for refusing to implicate others. He wrote two autobiographical books about his experiences, the last one entitled *Redhanded*.

Although the accelerated Master's of Social Work program that Kay and I took began in September of 1944 and finished in January of 1946, the degree was not formally granted until 1948, after the school officially became part of McGill University. For my first-year field placement, I went to the Montreal Neurological Institute, where I obtained a full-time job after finishing my degree. As we approached graduation, our class was determined to raise the pitiful salary levels in social work. We held meetings at which we decided we would, one and all, hold firm for a starting salary of $1,500 a year, or $300 over the existing rate. The manoeuvre was successful due to the keen desire for social workers at the time, and had the fortunate effect of also bumping up salaries for more senior positions.

At first I was a caseworker, trying to help individual patients and their families solve or improve whatever problems existed in their social situation that was often further complicated by illness. I was very much in awe of most of the world-renowned doctors at the Neurological Institute: Penfield, Cone, Elvidge, and McNaughton. I could barely stand to watch a brain operation, something others seemed to handle with abandon while I felt continually in danger of fainting. From time to time I suffered the symptoms of the most complex neurological illnesses, be it muscular dystrophy, multiple sclerosis, or one of those more obscure and difficult to diagnose. The head nurse, Eileen Flanagan, was to me a terrifying and sarcastic pit bull, but my boss, the director of social work, was a dear woman, kind, warm, and loving. Mrs. Davidson was a Southern belle from Georgia who became something of a mother-substitute after my own mother died of a stroke in 1948. Later she agreed to be god-mother to my daughter, although by the time Glynnis was born, Mrs. Davidson had left Montreal and returned to the southern United States.

My last year at the Neuro was spent doing a research study with some of our clinic patients on the social problems of epilepsy at home, in school, and in the community. Mrs. Davidson was able to obtain funds from the Québec government to print the monograph. I wrote it, describing what we had learned working with Dr. Francis McNaughton. The whole purpose of the study was educational, to sensitize the public to the illness and bring greater understanding and acceptance.

After the war ended, there was an agonizing eight-month wait before Vincent's unit returned to Canada and he was demobilized.

We had concocted a plan with some teachers I knew that he would enroll in the School of Art and Design at the Art Association of Montreal (later the Montreal Museum of Fine Arts), where he could explore his artistic gifts. The three-year program would be paid by the government's free educational entitlement for those veterans who did not want to settle on a farm.

Finally reunited in Montreal, Vincent and I found that living in the housing co-op was not suitable for a couple trying to revive their marriage after a long separation. There were too many meetings and too much interpersonal conflict. We found an apartment in the Snowdon area and began our married life for the second time, Vincent as a student at art school and I as a social worker.

Although we had sent very regular short blue airmail letters, living together was another story. We had to get to know one another anew. I had new friends now. It was a new city to him as well. Fortunately, his fellow students were a congenial bunch and most of them were veterans as well. It was a stimulating period for the teachers who enjoyed the older students with their life experience and commitment.

CHAPTER FIVE

Jacknife Lodge

IN 1946, VINCENT AND I took our first summer holiday, biking from Ottawa to Algonquin Park where we rented a canoe for a week-long camping trip. It was great fun despite the many long hills we had to climb before we reached Canoe Lake. Each night we were able to find a campsite with fresh water, our basic requirement.

During the next winter in Montreal, we thought a great deal about how to construct a future life that would have some economic security. Much as he was enjoying his art courses and doing well in the three-year program, it seemed unlikely that he could ever be able to make a livelihood from painting. Owning and operating a summer resort in cottage country had been a dream in the back of his mind for years. We decided to see if we could bring it to fruition in my beloved Georgian Bay, and the next summer vacation we drove there to begin work on our plan. En route we checked with the Ontario Department of Lands and Forests in Parry Sound, to find out what land was available for purchase from the Crown. A small peninsula of seven acres with many feet of indented shoreline offered what seemed to be an ideal site, even though there was no road access for the final quarter mile. During the 1947 and 1948 summer vacations we both did backbreaking work as long as there was any daylight, hauling rock from nearby shores, splitting it and making endless quantities of mortar to build the foundation for the main building, to create a large outdoor patio, and finally to build a stone

[top] The framework of the main house goes up at Jacknife.
[bottom] Vincent and Joan putting on roof boards.

[top] Left to right: Leslie Thomas (Vincent's brother), John Carter (Joan's brother), Vincent, Kay Percival, and Ed Percival.
[bottom] The main building completed, c. 1951.

chimney nearly two meters wide, with fireplaces inside and out.

One night in February of 1948 we were awakened with the news that my mother had died in her sleep from a stroke. She had suffered from high blood pressure for years and we did not yet have effective drugs for that condition. I went to Toronto for the funeral, but apart from the sadness that such an occasion provokes I really did not feel a great loss. Somehow the split had come earlier. She was sixty-two years of age. This seemed so much older than my father had been— forty-nine—at his death that it did not seem unusual to me that she should succumb. In fact, I felt a sense of relief that the stroke had been fatal and had not heralded a long incapacity.

The following year I did feel regret that my mother would never meet my daughter, Glynnis Margaret, whose second name was chosen in memory of her. Although the discovery that I was pregnant had been somewhat unexpected, we were excited by the prospect and determined that this need not change our long-term plans. Vincent had finished his art course and with the baby due in early October, I resigned from my job at the Montreal Neurological Institute in June and we headed back to Georgian Bay. Very soon the wooden structure of the main cabin took shape. My mother's death had brought me a small inheritance, sufficient to finish the main house and then three small sleeping cabins and a utility building for laundry. For financial reasons it was important to open, at least minimally, the following season. We decided to spend the whole of the coming winter at the lodge doing work on the interior and building furniture in order to be prepared to receive a few guests.

On October 7, 1949, our daughter was born in Toronto's Grace Hospital. Followers of Dr. D. Grantley Read's book on natural childbirth, we had intended my delivery to be in Parry Sound but two brief admissions to hospital during the summer for what turned out to be a minor problem had frightened me and convinced us that we wanted the best big-city care. I was greatly relieved when my brother-in-law, himself a doctor, made all the arrangements.

After leaving the hospital, Glynnis, Vincent, and I spent Glynnis' first six weeks at my sister's home in Toronto. With three children of her own at the time, Mary was helpful and reassuring as I attempted to learn how to care for an infant, and I was grateful for her hospitality. Then we hastened to get settled in back up north before winter arrived. Much remained to be done if we were to survive it.

The snow had not yet arrived so we were able to drive over the rocks to within a hundred yards of the lodge. We stocked up on staples from the nearest town because it would only be in late January or February that the ice would become thick and hard enough to drive over to our door. I remember carrying a fifty-pound bag of flour on my back for those last hundred yards and thinking that this was probably not something the medical profession would have recommended at six weeks post-partum. To buy fresh food, one of us would have to ski about a mile to the house of our helpful neighbours, give them our shopping list and return a day later with a backpack.

Our first consideration was heating. The building was not insulated and it had a lot of glass and only a single layer of wood sheathing. Our solution was one much used in the north in those days. We purchased an old empty 45-gallon oil drum, took it to a machine shop, had them cut a hole in one end and fit a stove door on it with another hole in the top for a stove pipe. Stubby legs were attached and presto! we had a ready-made stove. We had to remove a window pane to make the exit hole for the stove pipe. It worked well although at times it was a source of anxiety when it became red-hot after being loaded up with logs at bedtime. The fire never lasted through the night and always had to be remade by whomever crawled out of a chilly bed first in the morning.

We spent a great deal of time sawing and splitting wood for our two ravenous stoves. We had a Québec heater in the kitchen that we lit in the morning and that served as our cookstove. We also used it to heat water for sponge baths and laundry. There was of course no running water, just the buckets carried up from the lake. Pails of diapers were constantly stewing away on the stove. There were no disposable diapers in those days, and we certainly had no washing machine. Later we acquired one that ran on gasoline and was started by stepping with great force on a foot-pedal as many times as needed to get it going. There was something very satisfying about bringing in the wash from the line, frozen stiff, with a gorgeous, fresh smell. Meanwhile, the chairs, tables and benches were emerging slowly. Our time horizon seemed endless since there was no pressure. Deadlines for accomplishing each task had to be self-imposed, and we created minor ones to help us keep a sense of purpose in our lives.

For water, we used an axe to maintain an opening in the lake about 18 inches square (about half a square meter) a short distance from the shore. During the coldest months, this meant chopping it every day so the frozen layer on top did not get too thick. By late winter when it was ice-cutting time for all the residents on the Bay, the ice layer was about eighteen inches deep. A man living in the area came with his team of horses, ice saws, awl, and a sleigh. He cut a large patch in the ice, sawed it into blocks and took it to our icehouse to be stored in sawdust, where we would use it all summer. The ice was essential because without electricity all our perishable food had to be kept in iceboxes during the warmer months.

It was a healthy life. Germs did not seem to exist and we never had so much as a head cold. With a new, first baby this was a definite plus. A total greenhorn, I knew only what I read in Dr. Benjamin Spock's invaluable baby-bible. Life would have been far more difficult had Glynnis not been so healthy, since there were no doctors or knowledgeable females nearby. I worried when her crying seemed excessive, but it passed and signified nothing serious. Nursing her, I sometimes felt unsure whether she was getting enough milk and would have welcomed a visit from a member of the La Leche League had there been one there! Glynnis required an inoculation at three months of age. I had been given instructions by our doctor in

Toronto. One practiced on an orange, because its peel has about the same resistance as human skin. Inserting a syringe into an orange and into a baby are quite different procedures, however, and when I managed to do it successfully I felt a great sense of relief.

This was a long winter. Our lives were rather lonely but there were compensations in the simple things like looking out our front window to watch an otter amusing himself by sliding down a steep rock near the house. Periodically the ice would emit a huge boom that sounded very ominous but had no apparent effect, and was probably related to expansion and contraction. I remember one incredibly beautiful night, windless with a moon and northern lights in the sky. We decided to go out for a brief walk on the ice. The baby was sleeping soundly and we left her behind. We did not go very far or stay out very long. I was haunted by the fear that something unforeseen would happen to us, and I imagined Glynnis slowly dying of hunger in her crib. It was the only occasion on which one of us was not with her.

Another worry was driving on the ice. We waited until one of the local people had made the track, a route based on long experience that avoided those parts of the Bay where the current kept the ice from freezing hard. Still, we never felt completely safe, and when we first made the crossing, I kept the door of the truck open, with Glynnis in my arms, ready to jump should I hear any ice cracking. But being able to get out together and visit with acquaintances along the road helped us to avoid cabin fever. Parry Sound was our closest town for food or other supplies.

I learned from experience that one does actually walk in a circle when lost. I had never believed this, or thought that if one was aware of the tendency, one could easily counteract it by conscious effort. Not so. On one occasion when I went out for supplies, I took a different route back that had no visual markers. I was completely astonished to discover that, despite my efforts, I did make a huge circle. Fortunately I was soon able to spot a recognizable landmark

Joan and Glynnis in 1952. (Unknown person in rear.)

and made my way home.

In late March, before the ice gave way and the road turned into a sea of mud, we left for a month's holiday in Toronto. At first we experienced considerable culture shock, but we soon found it a great relief to see and talk to friends. Later, when our marriage broke up, there were some who felt that our isolation had set the stage irrevocably for our separation, though this was not my perception. At any event, we did not spend another winter up north. We spent the following two winters in Toronto, the first one in a cottage on the outskirts of the city, on Scarborough Bluffs. Our rented home was inadequately heated by an oil-guzzling space heater. There were no neighbours and Vincent drove off at 7 a.m. in the truck to do painting or carpentry in the city, returning after 6 o'clock. It seemed to be a different kind of isolation than we had experienced up north and I was extremely lonely. The second winter we tried to make better plans and shared a house in Willowdale with a couple and their two-year-old daughter. It was less lonely but not really satisfactory because, among other things, I found it hard to accept frequent spanking of the child. Each spring we exulted when we were able to return to the Bay.

The next two summers passed without incident. We continued building sleeping cabins. During the first year a few people we knew arrived as paying guests. I took on the cooking and the other kitchen chores with the help of something called "Basic Mix", an amalgam of flour, salt, and baking powder which could be turned quickly into dumplings, cakes, puddings, or tea biscuits. No one starved, but neither did anyone urge me to remain as chief cook.

The second summer we felt we could afford to hire a cook since we had more guests and friends from the art communities of both Montreal and Toronto. We hired a woman who had spent the winter cooking in a lumber camp in the north. She unfortunately had a taste for the bottle. On her day off to visit her home in Parry Sound she would fail to return, and one of us would have to drive into town and bring her back to the lodge to recover from her hangover.

It was during our third summer at Jacknife that my life would turn upside-down.

Joan working on the framing.

CHAPTER SIX

End of a Marriage

IN THE SUMMER OF 1952, Vincent invited Goodridge Roberts, one of his teachers at the Art School, to visit us at Jacknife Lodge. He had often spoken enthusiastically to me and to others about Goodridge, mentioning his admiration for both the man and his work. I had met him *en passant* at a student party several years before, where Mavis Gallant was also a guest. She had complained about people whose marriages break up but who go on endlessly talking about their former partners. It had been obvious to everyone that she was talking about Goodridge, and I was annoyed at her pointing the finger at him in this way, but I later learned that her own marriage had recently ended. I learned much later too, with pleasure, that she was very fond of Goodridge's work and had sacrificed, in those early years, to buy a small painting, paying with small payments over a considerable period of time. Her good friend had done the same, and when she died she left Mavis her Roberts since Mavis had regretfully been unable to retain hers.

When Goodridge arrived at Jacknife, he had been divorced from his wife Marian for six years, but he was still unhappy and inclined to feel guilty about the failure of his marriage. Vincent urged me to be kind and understanding. He came with Alfred Pinsky, a fellow artist from Montreal, and they planned to spend six weeks with us, painting outdoors. With a few other bookings in hand, we felt the lodge was beginning to be viable as a business.

From the beginning, Goodridge's painting went well, seemingly unaffected by any gloom he might have been feeling. Once he had worked out his schedule, become settled and familiar with his surroundings, he managed to complete two oils every day. I thought they were impressive, as was his commitment to his work. As he trudged back from his outings to his cabin on the point, carrying his folding easel, knapsack of paints, and the Masonite board on which he had just completed a picture, he seemed to take pleasure in showing his paintings to anyone who happened to be around.

I loved his work and the feeling and sensitivity it demonstrated. His paintings were no mere decorative depictions of rocks and water, but to me statements about life and about himself. Perhaps I fell in love with the works first, but to me they seemed inseparable from the man who had created them.

As the days turned into weeks we found that we were spending more and more time with each other. Vincent and I always ate our meals with the guests. Sometimes we all took a picnic to some other island where Goodridge and I would manage to find excuses to be alone together. By the end of the season and after Alfie Pinsky had left Jacknife to return to Montreal, the unintended consequence of our summer was that we realized that we were in love and had become deeply committed to one another. Some powerful need in me had been met by both the man and his work. This created an incredibly complex situation and as the last guests left in late August, Goodridge and I attempted to put off any decision about what we should do, but this proved impossible.

One day, Vincent confronted me about the extent of our intimacy. I was unable to deny it, and told him the truth, that we were very much in love. His reaction was fury, unforgiving and relentless. He refused to discuss anything and in fact took off almost immediately in the truck. We did not know where he had gone or for how long but there were things that had to be attended to at the lodge and so we carried on as normally as possible. When he did return in two or three days, we learned he had been in Toronto, had seen his lawyer and my sister Mary, but he was even more inaccessible than before, refusing to discuss anything, a means of working things out, or what would happen to Glynnis. Raving like a madman, he precipitated the break by ordering Goodridge and me to leave the property immediately. He seemed to be so close to violence that I was terrified for us all.

His behaviour became even more deranged when I said that I wanted to take Glynnis with me. I was aware that Glynnis, like myself, counted as one of his possessions. I did not fear that he would harm her in any way, no matter how he was acting, since I felt sure that his state of mind was temporary and I hoped that soon he would come to his senses. I also knew that he could, and I felt would, give her very good care. And for her sake, I thought he would eventually let her stay with me even if he and I were unable to reach some kind of reconciliation. His frame of mind at that particular time was so extreme, however, that I was truly afraid that he might run amok and kill both Goodridge and me, and we decided we had to get away from him.

That night, Goodridge and I left under cover of darkness. I remember creeping down the road to a place a considerable distance from the Lodge so that he could pick me up in his car on the chance that, if Vincent tried to follow, he would think that Goodridge was leaving alone. I got in beside him and waited for my heart to stop pounding as we began the long drive from Jacknife Lodge to Montreal.

We drove to Montreal without stopping, ending up at the home of our friends, the Polands, who put us up for the night. Our plan was to continue on the next day to Québec City, where Goodridge would leave me with a good friend of mine who lived there. I was to stay with her for as long as it took to consider the situation calmly and work out what action should follow. But as we drove out of Montreal we had barely arrived at the outskirts when the car gave a mighty groan and died on the spot. We learned that repairs would take several days, so we had to change our plans and return to our friends. We never did get to Québec City. Instead, we decided that if we were going to be in Montreal for some time, we had better find accommodation for both of us there. We located a two-room apartment with kitchenette at 1300 Pine Avenue overlooking the city, just below the mountain.

Soon the consternation and reproof over my separation from Vincent and my child began to pour in from family and friends. In the context of those times, it was almost unheard-of for women to leave their husbands or young children. They accused me of giving in to a passing infatuation and urged me to return to Vincent. The letters and phone calls hurt even more because I shared many of their concerns and could not expect them to understand what this relationship meant to me. After a few weeks, Vincent did make some attempts at reconciliation, but they were so laden with blame and his unconcealed desire to make me suffer intense guilt and punishment that they were futile. Equally futile were my efforts to persuade him to let Glynnis, not quite three years old, live with Goodridge and me.

As a result, those first days in Montreal were perhaps the most difficult I have ever spent. It was an untenable situation and I felt totally powerless. I was being torn apart between my love for Goodridge and my grief at being separated from my child. Faced with the prospect of living without her, I was unable to conceive what course the rest of my life would take. My unhappiness was such that it was unclear whether our relationship could survive. That such difficult times existed for women in my situation is almost unimaginable now with all that has happened to improve women's rights, not to mention how very common marriage breakdown has become. Undoubtedly my inability to see Glynnis continued to be the most difficult aspect of our life together. When Vincent could be persuaded to let me have any contact with her, he was able to lay the ground rules as to where any visit would take place, who would be present, and how long it would last, and I was always told that if I did not abide by these rules, this would be the last time I would see her. He allowed me to have three short visits in different places, so I travelled to Toronto, to St. Catharines in southern Ontario and to Georgian Bay to be with her. Goodridge was never to be with me. Each parting from her was agonizing.

I did not know which way to turn. Despite my strong feelings of guilt, I could not convince myself that if I just returned to live with Vincent, as he and my sister advised, all would be well. By now he had hurt me too much with everything he had said, and I knew that he would continue wanting to make me suffer for my misdeeds. In addition to threatening to come to Montreal to kill Goodridge, he had made a huge bonfire and burnt all my books and university notes, my clothing, keepsakes and other belongings which I had not taken with me that fateful night. He stipulated in a very nasty letter the only conditions under which he would consider proceeding with his action to divorce me. First, I had to give up the claim to custody of Glynnis that I had filed. Secondly, I had to relinquish legally any interest or ownership in the Lodge, including the money I had put into it from the beginning. I felt at a complete impasse because, without a divorce that would give me legal rights, I was at Vincent's mercy regarding parental visits. Added to my sense of guilt over having left my child was the difficulty of accepting what had happened to the man I had once loved.

Over time, however, Vincent's harassment only seemed to deepen the love and trust I felt for Goodridge. During those difficult days he was unfailingly supportive and loving without pressuring me toward any decision I might make, no matter what the outcome might be. On one of the occasions when I went to visit Glynnis, he wrote in a letter to me:

> You have made life more wonderful for me than anyone
> else ever has or could have, and I don't think that even if I

were to be deprived of your presence forever I could ever again find another who could give me such joy.... I want to dedicate all the parts and qualities of myself to telling you of my love. I want to paint for you. I want to be a better man for you.... If you can be by my side for the rest of life that will be the greatest blessing but with me in person or not how can there be any place in my heart, so filled as it is with the joy of our love, for anyone else?

His steadfast support gave me the strength to go on and to try to live as normal a life as possible. I was also helped by the kindness of good friends in Montreal, even though my sense of loss was such that it remained a physical one, a pain that nothing could eliminate or even alleviate.

I tried to ease my sense of loss in various ways. I took a part-time job and was grateful always to the woman who hired me and who had refrained from comments about my living with a man who was not my husband. I sought advice and counselling from Dr. Prados, the well-known psychiatrist who knew Goodridge and who had been one of my teachers. I made a few new friends in Montreal and tried to live as normal a social life as possible. I also explored my legal rights. I travelled to Toronto for a visit with the professional in the Official Guardian's office, but she had no intention of seeing me before making her recommendation about custody to the judge as required in Ontario. As far as she was concerned, I was the one who had left, and that was enough: I was the "scarlet woman" and deserved my fate. I even made another special trip to Toronto to talk to the woman Vincent was by then planning to marry, in order to plead with her for help in persuading Vincent to let Glynnis live with me, but of course she would not go against his wishes.

Through this whole time I tried to believe that my marriage must have been shaky and that something in it must have been lacking or I could not have fallen in love with another man so easily.

I will never know whether this was actually true or an attempt at self-justification. Possibly the outcome might have been different if Vincent had not behaved so badly, but I was positive that I could not give up Goodridge in order to spend the rest of my life with Vincent. Twelve months passed, and he continued his abuse until I capitulated and agreed to give up my claim for custody after learning from a lawyer in my father's firm who reviewed the file for me that my chances of success were almost nil.

The divorce hearing was held in St. Catharines. It was Vincent's official residence and where his family lived. Just before the date my lawyer told me that he thought it would be better if I pleaded my own case for visitation rights of fifty days per year during school holidays rather than having him present in court. I was told that Vincent was asking the judge to allow me no rights of visitation at all, that I should be dead to all intents and purposes as far as Glynnis was concerned.

Although the hearing was a huge ordeal and I was frightfully nervous on the stand, I managed to get through it. The horror of my situation was compounded, however, when the judge told Vincent and me that he wanted us to go out to lunch together to try to break the impasse and come up with a visitation plan we could both accept. I felt that my future was on the line, dependent upon my powers of persuasion. One minute Vincent would agree with me, and the next he would revert to his starting point, angrier than ever. Nonetheless, for some reason the judge gave me what I asked for, although it was not what I really wanted. A *decree nisi* was granted and the final divorce would be granted six months later. Until then, there was no legal requirement to allow me visiting time.

CHAPTER SEVEN

Goodridge

WHO WAS THIS MAN who, without intending it, had brought so much turmoil into our lives? My first impression was of someone tall and handsome, whose gaze, when our eyes met, conveyed deep under-standing and acceptance. To those who did not know him well, he was a quiet man, fond of reading and writing poetry, a shy introvert who preferred to do quick sketches of friends rather than participate in a discussion or argument. His colleague, the artist Jacques de Tonnancour, once likened him to a sleepwalker, having to improvise his life because he had no technique for tackling its practicalities. But to his friends and family members he was known for a sense of humour that welcomed the absurdities and incongruities of human nature, and added them to an ever-growing fund of stories he loved to tell. His sense of humour was an important leavening feature of our life together. We shared a sense of the absurd and his unerring command of the English language made his stories memorable. I never failed to be impressed by his unfailing ability to choose exactly the right word or phrase.

Goodridge the man, as I perceived him, was inseparable from Goodridge Roberts the artist. In his work, he maintained an almost symbiotic relationship with his subject. He always had an intensely close interaction with whatever he saw and this meant that he never worked on a landscape unless he could actually see it—which is why most of his winter landscapes were done from a window. He always worked rapidly and with intensity, so that no matter how large it was, three to four hours would bring the painting to completion, for better or worse. Paintings were not reworked a second day, with the exception of the occasional figure work. Instead, if he felt that something was a clear failure, he would scrape it off and begin again, not wanting to waste the masonite. Apart from those rare occasions, he seldom destroyed a painting, and would say of his limited successes, "Well, I guess it has something."

Occasionally he would fret about his inability to paint except with the subject in front of him. Success using photographs proved equally elusive, and the few paintings he attempted in this way did not turn out well. When he was in England as a war artist with the Royal Canadian Air Force he had difficulty doing anything except drawings of the servicemen on the bases or bleak watercolours of the airfields and hangars. Some official suggested that photographs would be of assistance and he was supplied with a photographer to journey with him from base to base for a couple of weeks. The photographer took hundreds of shots, but despite Goodridge's embarrassment at how much this must cost and his desire to justify it, he was unable to use a single one.

On the other hand, in earlier years he had done dozens of pencil and ink drawings conjured up entirely out of his imagination, all of them with humorous or satirical subjects. Once he tried to turn a couple of these early drawings into paintings, but they could not have satisfied him because he never continued this kind of work. In the early 1930s he did a stage set at Queen's University for T.S. Eliot's *Murder in the Cathedral* and in the late '40s he submitted a painting of a lynching to the Spring Show at the Art Association of Montreal. When it came back, he tried to work on it further, felt he had spoiled it, and ended up over-painting it with the "Interior" now in the Hamilton Art Gallery. Later he wished that he had preserved the original and wondered if his earlier evaluation had been accurate. These, though, are about the only examples of pictures not painted

Goodridge served as a war artist in England, 1943-45.

directly from a subject, even with his largest works.

Unless he was working close to home, most of his painting involved considerable physical labour. During a stay at the farm that we eventually bought, I remember him carrying his folding easel, paints, brushes, and a 29 x 36-inch (about 72 x 90 cm) board to a spot nearly half a mile away with no road access. The walk home involved two trips, one carrying only a single wet painting that he tried to keep from being touched by bushes and the underbrush, and the other for his painting supplies. On one occasion, during a stay in the Laurentians in 1953, he became lost and wandered through the bush for an hour until he reached a road and was able to orient himself; he was fortunate to have only a relatively small painting attached to his folding easel.

From the beginning, our relationship seemed to be a close one. I felt an enormous trust in him and I think he did in me as well. We were both relaxed and caring with each other, even though we knew so little about each other's life up to our point of meeting. There was a lot of sharing between us, and neither of us held back incidents or feelings. We quickly forged an intimacy that was strong and sustaining.

I not only liked the way he treated me, with respect and consideration, but the way he treated others. I never knew him to denigrate a woman in any way. There was an honesty and integrity and a profound humanity in him that I had not encountered before with anyone else.

Shortly after we had moved into our Pine Avenue apartment, Goodridge found in a studio on Beaver Hall Hill an easel that had belonged to Horne Russell, a Scottish-born artist of some renown in the first part of the twentieth century. It served its purpose well, particularly after we lugged it up to the apartment building's roof deck so Goodridge could do several paintings overlooking the city (one of which is now in the Québec Museum), but it was so massive and heavy that we had to abandon it when we gave up the apartment.

I was often struck by the degree to which my outlook on a variety of situations was similar to Goodridge's, despite our different backgrounds. But my understanding of people and their behaviour had been hard won with years of formal study, whereas Goodridge seemed to arrive at the same point by intuition. So we did not need to have disputes about values, attitudes, or even motives very often. More often than not we agreed and I found him very easy to live with. I regretted that he did not have any interest in physical activity apart from walking but he did not mind me engaging in sports when I wanted.

While not formally political, he had a strong sense of social justice and the need for social change. Like most English-speaking artists and intellectuals in Montreal in the pre-war and post-war period, he identified with the progressive left. This did not stop him from recounting with amusement how a woman who was well-known as a communist went to see an exhibition of his watercolour landscapes at the McGill Faculty Club. She spent a good bit of time looking and, obviously wanting to find something positive to say, finally came up with the statement that she could just imagine Stalin peering out from behind a certain bush. The most public, political act that I remember was his accepting to be a member of a committee of well-known people who lobbied to overturn Duplessis' infamous Padlock Law. Artists were often asked to contribute paintings to raise funds for one or another cause, sometimes giving outright and some-times retaining a small percentage if the painting sold. Goodridge and many others did that for the Spanish Civil War.

The other intellectual thread for Montreal anglophone artists in the 1950s was psychoanalysis. This was in large part due to the arrival in the city of Dr. Miguel Prados. He had come in the early '40s, I believe at the invitation of Dr. Wilder Penfield. He was a sensitive, cultured, and progressive Spanish psychoanalyst who brought a new excitement to the art scene and who became a kind of guru for many artists, tending as he did to move in the same social circles. I was told that his brother, a poet living in Mexico, was encouraged and supported by Prados much in the manner of Theo and Vincent Van Gogh. Goodridge was amongst the artists who saw him professionally for several years after the breakup of his first marriage, paying with paintings when money was scarce. A copy of Giotto's "Deposition" done by Goodridge was one of these. It was sold back to our family after both Prados and his daughter had died.

Prados had, of course, been a much respected teacher of mine at McGill and when Goodridge and I first were together, I consulted him about our relationship, given the anguish I was feeling. In true psychoanalytic fashion, he did not say much, as I remember, but I think the fact that he did not condemn me must have been greatly reassuring. I also recall he felt that we had a better chance of success at our ages of thirty and forty-eight than had we been twenty and thirty-eight.

The need for analytic treatment as a pre-requisite for those in the helping professions was starting to be felt, and for this and other reasons I asked Prados for the name of an analyst he would recommend for me. An appropriate and talented young man was found and thus began in 1956 three years of thrice-weekly sessions at the end of my workdays, and Goodridge's initiation into preparing dinner. I had known too many persons who had been in analysis for seemingly endless years, so I made it a condition that I would not come for more than three years. I was a bit surprised that this was accepted, but it became a given. Goodridge always had dinner ready when I finally got home but we ate minute steak, frozen squash, and frozen potato puffs more often than I care to remember. I think psychoanalysis helped me generally, although one of my goals took a long time to reach: it would be a great many years before I would overcome my uncomfortable stage fright when speaking in public.

These were good years, though—productive and happy. His work was selling, he was continuing to have regular exhibitions in Montreal and Toronto, and he was invited to represent Canada internationally. In 1952 he was one of three Canadian artists selected for Canada's first participation in the Venice Biennale. Also in 1952 and in 1955 he had work chosen for the prestigious Carnegie International at Pittsburgh. In 1958 he had works in the Inter-American Biennial of Painting in Mexico and in the same year his paintings were exhibited at the Brussels World's Fair. Occasionally there would be an award or prize which would please him and give him increased confidence in his work.

It has often been remarked that Goodridge disliked teaching art though it was financially necessary for him to do it for many years. Goodridge said he disliked it because he did not want to discourage a student and yet was unable to encourage work he considered unworthy of praise. On one occasion he thought he had made a breakthrough in this educational stalemate when he came back from lunch and discovered what he felt was a truly bad drawing. He found himself expressing his deep reservations to the student, who told him with a smirk that Arthur Lismer, the school's director, had done it while Goodridge was out for lunch. He probably did not have much to say for a good while. Another story he told about his teaching concerned a student he noted was back in class after an absence. Pleased with his observation he said to her, "You have been away". "Yes," she replied, "for seven years".

To counterbalance this aspect of his skills as a teacher, it must be emphasized that he inspired many students and young artists with his disciplined attitude to his work, his integrity, and his undeviating commitment to painting. His students felt his influence by example, almost by osmosis and there were a good number who went on to succeed in this relentless occupation: John Fox, Jeanne Rheaume, Paterson Ewen, Bill Kinnis, Jacques de Tonnancour, Georges de Niverville, Ghitta Caiserman-Roth, and Robert Roussill, to mention a few. What he did not convey of technique, he more than made up in inspiration. A senior artist, Catherine Bates, who is exhibiting now in 2009, in her catalogue credits Goodridge Roberts for her inspiration in landscape painting.

While often considered to be solitary and unsociable, particularly in earlier years, that is not at all how I remember him during our days in Montreal. Even though he might cross the street to avoid the approach of someone he knew who might corner him, he still used to like to go out after his day's work was completed and have tea at the Miss Westmount, a local restaurant where many of the same people gathered each day and where the friendly owner, Shirley, a woman expansive in size and manner, kept track of the health and problems of her customers. Often he arranged to see friends in the evening. Small gatherings at people's homes were a feature of the fifties, when we would meet and converse with friends. They included Philip and Margaret Surrey, John Fox and Louise Cass, Stanley Cosgrove, Alf Pinsky and Ghitta Caiserman, Betty and Martin Goodwin, Françoise Sullivan and Paterson Ewen, Neufville Shaw, Allan Harrison, as well as many others in the art and intellectual community. While Goodridge did not get into discussions of politics or art theories, he loved to regale any gathering with his amusing stories of events that had befallen him and which often had a bizarre, or at the very least, a paradoxical touch. He played bridge and every now and then we would enjoy a game with friends. He loved watching the Montreal Canadiens play on Saturday night TV and once turned away a man who said he wanted to buy a painting, but had rung the doorbell without an appointment during a game.

I believe that Goodridge's imagination was fed by poetry most of all. He rarely read novels when I knew him, but he always had a book of poetry handy. At first it would probably have been Spender, Auden, Yeats, or Eliot, but he seemed to be aware somehow of the latest writings in English and we had tiny chapbooks of people like Alan Ginsberg and Lawrence Ferlinghetti. How the transfer from poetry to painting occurred in his imagination and creativity I cannot say, but certainly poetry was vital to him. Curiously, perhaps, he did not read art criticism, and art books were in our library in order for him to peruse the reproductions. He did enjoy reading, but his preference always was for essays and poetry. While he did not write poetry when I knew him, he had done so in his younger years. One couplet which reveals his playful sense of humour and which I particularly like is:

Cézanne at last was tempted by an apple,
To forego women and with fruit to grapple.

CHAPTER EIGHT

Saskatoon and the Seagram Project

IN DECEMBER OF 1952, just a few months after Goodridge and I had begun our lives together in Montreal, he learned of a project organized by Seagram's Limited to commission ten Canadian artists to paint each one of Canada's provincial capitals. The company would retain everything that was painted, and they would form Seagram's "Cities of Canada Collection". Responsibility for implementing the project was entrusted to the advertising firm Vickers and Benson.

I cannot say how the chosen artists were assigned their cities, but Goodridge was asked to paint Saskatoon, a place where he had never set foot. He had many misgivings, but the remuneration was quite substantial, too much for us, given our circumstances, to refuse. Another thing that concerned him was that this was a commission, and he was unsure that he could paint a subject to order. The time frame must have been very short for him to choose to go off a few days after Christmas in the depths of a prairie winter. The only solution was to work from a window in the Bessborough Hotel overlooking the river and a part of the city.

He describes the experience in letters he wrote to me:

> The plane trip [his first] was a peculiar experience ... the noise of the engines was terrific! There wasn't any feeling of exhilaration as there was no sense of speed at all at the altitude we travelled. In fact I kept thinking that we must

be going too slowly to continue to stay up. The countryside from up there looked as flat as a pancake, and the patterns made by fields, lakes and what-not interested me even less than a picture by Gordon Webber [an artist and design teacher at the Museum School of Art and McGill School of Architecture].

As you can tell by the letterhead, this is just another of those C.N.R. hotels. Anyway it's warm so I spent a number of hours today peering out of my bedroom window at a bit of Saskatoon and painting away on a 12" x 16". Tomorrow I shall get a larger canvas and do the same scene on it, then try to arrange to get a room on a higher floor and another exposure and repeat the performance.

I can't quite make up my mind whether the thing I did today is a sort of Clarence Gagnon Christmas card or something better. Anyway I worked hard at it and with some pleasure. The fact that it is full of houses, snow, people and churches and all kinds of colours should make it highly acceptable to Vickers and Benson...

I did another 12" x 16" today from the same window. It turned out pretty well I think. ...The one I did yesterday has its points too. It took me about four hours to do each of them. After finishing today's sketch I went out to find some canvas. Couldn't get any stretcher pieces to make up a 23" x 32" canvas but managed to get their alternative size, 30" x 40", and have just finished sketching it. Tomorrow I shall do the same bloody scene on this scale and the next day try to get another room where I shall do one small and one large. Then call a halt and pull out ... with no regrets...

I moved into another room today and have just finished the other 30" x 40". It is really good. I feel a bit dubious about the others but this one is up to my successful summer ones. It's a great relief to discover that I can turn out something presentable when working to order like this. I guess old Doc Prados will have to concede that I'm making progress.

My letters up to now have been written when I felt comparatively cheerful. Now I am in the dumps. You won't mind if I tell you that I am. After all a man, to be a man, doesn't always have to feel strong and hopeful, or if he does feel otherwise have to hide it from his beloved....So this is New Years' Eve!

I went to a show tonight—a feeble comedy with Bob Hope and Bing Crosby. ...

~

New Years' Day—
Today I repainted the first large picture—even though I was in a different room from when I worked on it first. However, as I am just next door to my old place and have one window overlooking the same area, it was OK. I think I improved it.

This then was the Seagram story. We ran into the Collection in Paris, France the next year, where it was on tour with much pomp and hoopla. As Goodridge was the only Seagram artist in Paris, they urged, pleaded, cajoled him to be present at the opening. I think he had to rent a tuxedo for the occasion. Although my unmarried status had caused no particular notice in France until that point, this was a Canadian event and it was not socially acceptable for an unmarried partner to be included in invitations to social events and so I was not included, but the National Guard was. Attending the vernissage was one of the many times when Goodridge did something he really didn't want to. His Protestant guilt was as hard to shake as mine.

Goodridge's father died rather suddenly from a heart attack on

February of 1953. While later I was to know his mother, at that point I had not met either parent, and we agreed that it did not seem appropriate for me to attend the funeral. Goodridge flew to St. John on the eve of the burial, catching the ferry next morning to Digby, where his parents were living at the time. Of this he wrote,

There was some difficulty about getting a room for me, and it was only on the third try that a vacant one was located. They must have just picked out keys at random because the boy who was delegated to show me to it first led me to the fifth floor and ushered me into one already protestingly occupied. Then down to the desk for another key, up to the sixth and into another occupied room; down again and finally to an empty one on the fourth. A dreary, dirty one at that, and without a bath to solace myself in.

After the funeral service in Digby, the body was brought to Fredericton for burial in the Poets' Corner. The service included a reading from one of his father's poems with a reference to birch trees trembling in a light air. According to Goodridge, it was a windless day until this line was read and then there was a sudden rustle of the branches as if nature was in tune. It was the stuff of mystery and eeriness that often tended to make a stronger impression on Goodridge than mere reality. He was not religious in the sense of following any organized religion but he did have a strong moral and spiritual side to his character. With two grandfathers who were clergymen it could hardly have been otherwise

When he returned home, apparently without any obvious conscious decision, he began to do a series of self-portraits during the next several weeks. Some writers have attributed psychological motives to this undertaking, perhaps accurately. To me some of the paintings expressed vulnerability as well as sadness and loneliness. Whatever the ambivalence and complexity of his feelings about his father, his death left Goodridge as the only male member of the family. Self-examination and a review of the past were inevitable and it was natural for him to conduct such an exploration through his painting.

As summer drew closer we found a cottage to rent between Mille Iles and Morin Heights in the Laurentians. The owners had built a second small house on their property and welcomed us as tenants. There was a small spring-fed lake and rolling hills and fields, making it good painting country for Goodridge. For me it was near enough to Montreal that I could go in to work a couple of days each week because after our return to Montreal, I had found a part-time job in medical social work at the Royal Victoria Hospital. Two kittens added bounce to our household.

CHAPTER NINE

Europe

A VERY OPPORTUNITY came up during that first year together, 1952-53, when Max Stern, owner of the Dominion Gallery, brought to our attention the possibility of applying for a Canadian Government Overseas Fellowship. These grants were adequately funded with monies the government had decided to use for fellowships in the arts since the money was in francs which were frozen in France. Had it not been for the grants, the thought of going abroad at the time would never have entered our heads, as we did not have any money apart from the $250 monthly stipend from the contract Goodridge had with Max, supplemented by the odd outside sale of one of Goodridge's paintings and my small salary as a part-time social worker. We were also involved in our very worrisome problems here at home. Nevertheless we decided that Goodridge should apply and see what happened.

By the time the news arrived that Goodridge had won the grant, one of our problems had reached some resolution. The divorce was not scheduled to be heard until the autumn of 1953 and would be final in the late spring of 1954. Only then would the visiting days take effect. We would be able to see Glynnis fifty days a year; she would come to stay with us for one month in the summer and a week each at Christmas and Easter. A winter in France seemed possible before the final decree of the divorce judgment would arrive.

The voyage over was on the *Ile de France,* a magnificent ship even in bleak November with the Atlantic stormy and skies a leaden grey. On arrival in Paris we were pleased to be met by Goodridge's friend and former student, the painter Georges de Niverville, who had reserved a room for us in the Regent's Hotel on the Left Bank. It was comfortable, and was our home for several weeks before we found a small, furnished apartment on rue d'Aumale near Montmartre. The flat consisted of one large room with a bed in an alcove, a small kitchen, and a bathroom, and it seemed luxurious by Paris housing standards of the time. The rent was $150 monthly, with central heating that had to be supplemented by a wood heater in the living room. Bundles of twigs and sticks to keep it going had to be carried home from the store. It was my job to attend to these details and keep the household going. It was just not part of Goodridge's universe, though he was always most willing to help. The bathroom and kitchen had no heat but we were infinitely luckier than our friends that unusually cold winter. They often found water left standing overnight turned to a solid block of ice by morning. Daylight was important since Goodridge wanted natural light for his work and there was only one window in the front of the main room which gave directly onto the street. The row of three-storey buildings across the narrow street reduced further what little light there was throughout the long, grey, Paris winter. Occasionally Goodridge had to paint with the electric lights on and it was routine for him to always set up his easel and still life as close to our ground floor window as he could get. Passersby on the street would often stop and peer over his shoulder at what was going on. Privacy and illumination were not possible at the same time.

When we turned the $6,000 grant into francs at the bank, it had amounted to more than one million old francs and we had felt exceedingly pleased and very rich. This did not last, however, and frequently our mood was as gloomy as the weather. We were both often homesick, missing the familiar things that give support to lives at difficult times. We missed Glynnis greatly, and while this had been true at home as well, it had a keener edge in foreign surroundings.

On the street in Paris, 1953.

Moments of wonder and excitement would sometimes be swept away with an inrush of desolation and a strong sense of inappropriateness. It was unfortunate that this year could not have occurred at a more tranquil time in our lives. Then we could have given our attention and appreciation unreservedly to the many new stimuli and opportunities we encountered abroad.

However, when Goodridge was engrossed in his work with his usual incredible concentration, he would seem to be in another world for hours at a time, removed from everyday cares in a way that I could only envy but never achieve. His capacity for total concentration when working was remarkable, a characteristic I always admired and respected. For my part, I found that I was fascinated with the city and kept busy with my daily grocery shopping and cooking, French lessons at the Alliance Française, reading or trips to the Poste Restante in hopes of mail.

Once we had settled into our apartment, our life in Paris was a very simple one of work and domesticity with frequent visits to museums. We spent a lot of time at the Louvre, the Jeu de Paume, the Musée d'Art Moderne, and private galleries. For Goodridge it was crucial to have these museums nearby so that he could see at first hand works that he had known only in reproduction. Often the scale of an actual painting was a complete shock, as it was so far removed from the impression he had formed from books. Colours, too, were a revelation compared with those in reproductions. It was a rich experience for him and for me an immersion in art history. His own work was beginning to gel with solid, rich, and glowing still lifes emerging one after the other. His best painting that year was done during that winter in Paris. It proved his contention that the best conditions for working did not necessarily bring the best results.

At Christmas we spent three weeks in London. Our stay there turned out to be a reunion for me with my brother and sister-in-law, John and Helen Carter, and for Goodridge an introduction to them and a reunion with his cousin, Archie MacDonald, the subject of many figure paintings Goodridge had done. Archie had left Montreal the previous year to spend a small inheritance studying at the Slade School of Art. This was a warm and friendly time, each of us getting to know family who were important to the other. London also offered more splendid galleries to be visited and paintings to be seen: the Turners and Constables, the Blakes at the British Museum and the Cézannes at the Courtauld Institute. Goodridge felt an affinity for the work of Matthew Smith and other contemporary British painters whose works we encountered. We visited one of the leading private dealers inquiring about a possible exhibition, but nothing came of it because we failed to follow up on it.

The weather in London was chill and damp. The shilling-eating heater in our modest hotel room soon made us long for our Paris faggot-fed stove that provided warmth higher than one's shins. We spent Christmas Day with my brother John and his wife Helen in an ancient, draughty mausoleum of a house where we had been invited to eat and share the dinner preparations. The stove was in the cellar and the sink was outside in the courtyard. Preparations seemed to go on forever, and by the time we carried the dinner up the long staircase, it was cold. Only our host's Great Dane could have enjoyed that Christmas dinner. He was favoured with the delicious-looking loaf of brown bread which we had been eyeing longingly all afternoon.

John Steegman, who was at that time Director of the Montreal Museum of Fine Arts, had kindly provided us with half a dozen letters of introduction to notable persons in various art institutions in London. Goodridge felt he could not refuse this well-intentioned gesture of John's, but neither could he see himself using them, whether to secure an advantage or to begin an unsought acquaintance. Someone else in Montreal, I remember, had also offered an introduction to Picasso and Goodridge refused that too, but for different reasons. Such an audience with Picasso would have implied that he was paying homage to that celebrated painter, and would have been an unnatural posture for him. Picasso was clearly not his kind of painter. His attitude reminded me of his story of meeting Mackenzie King in a field in Kingsmere in the '30s. King said, "I see you are painting." Goodridge replied, "Yes, I am"—and he couldn't think of anything else to say.

Our flight home to Paris on a small, two-engine, propeller plane was smoother than the hair-raising trip we had experienced going to London. To my great relief, our next journey, to Belgium and Holland, was by train. We knew no one in these countries and went only to see the paintings. The museum in Brussels proved a disappointment; it was unlit and the natural light was too dim to view the paintings properly. In Holland we visited Amsterdam, Rotterdam, and The Hague. I know it gave Goodridge tremendous satisfaction to see the many works of Rembrandt, for whom he had always had the greatest sympathy and admiration.

Our many acquaintances in Paris were usually other Canadians, largely French-speaking. Most of them, like ourselves, were there temporarily, often living in hotels and eking out their grants as long as possible. I think we all found it difficult to penetrate the Parisian world at that time, irrespective of the ability to speak French. My memory is that those Francophone friends who were there for short periods felt more alienated than the Anglophones, perhaps because their expectations had been different. I remember going to a movie one evening with Anne Hébert and also visiting Paul Vanier Beaulieu's studio in Montparnasse.

Someone important to us then was Colette Loranger, Jean Palardy's sister who had been living in Paris with her daughter for some years. We felt very much at home with her and frequent invitations to Sunday suppers helped to mitigate our homesickness. Goodridge loved her desserts, especially her Gâteau St. Honoré. He gave her the painting he had done one Sunday afternoon from her balcony which overlooked a square. It was reminiscent of Marquet's painting with its iron fretwork balconies and distinctive Paris lighting standards. Other Canadians I remember encountering were the poet Rina

Lasnier, writer and journalist Dominique Clift , Tobie and Herb Stein-house, artist and journalist, also Alfred Pellan, to mention just a few.

It was early March when the heavy, grey skies finally broke up. Even after all these years, I can vividly recall the sense of joy and promise of that day when snatches of blue sky and scudding white clouds appeared as we walked in the Tuileries. I cannot remember any other time when I was suddenly conscious that at that precise moment spring was approaching. It was our signal to pack up and head south. Italy was our next stop to be followed by a stay in the south of France until we returned to Canada the end of June. Our friend and fellow artist Stanley Cosgrove had written of a small hotel he had found on the Mediterranean coast at a small village called Agay near St. Raphael, and we decided to join him there. We hoped the winter weather would have retreated by then. Stanley spoke of the cold and the necessity of heating by igniting a pot of flammable liquid in the middle of the room every half hour, a dangerous remedy for the cold certainly.

We went first to Florence where we stayed with Goodridge's old friend Jeanne Rheaume. After studying with him in Montreal she went to live in Italy. She introduced us to Florence's many treasures and beauties, although she abstained from our visit to the Pitti Palace, well aware of the exhaustion involved in trying to view its collection in one visit. One fine Sunday morning she drove us to Sienna with its beautiful central plaza. Leaving by train for Rome, we arranged to stop at Assisi overnight to see the Giotto frescoes and at Arezzo for those of Piero della Francesca. These towns were magnificent and the combination of art and setting so completely satisfying that Rome proved an anti-climax. Somehow no experience in our brief stay there, including the Sistine Chapel, seemed to match those of the preceding days. We were definitely beginning to approach a state of surfeit. We stayed in a small *pensione* with ghastly meals. It was inhabited mainly by British tourists of limited means due to currency restrictions. I remember an amusing conversation with some of them one evening when the question was asked whether a certain painting had been in some church. The reply was that this week they were "only doing floors," so presumably they had not looked up.

Our last stop in Italy was for a week in Venice with a day trip to Padua to see the Piera della Francesca frescoes. Venice was a delight and we were thoroughly entranced with its beauty. It was neither crowded nor affected to any significant degree by the land sinking and pollution of more recent years. The spring weather was glorious and we walked along the streets and canals, basked in Piazza San Marco, visited the glassworks at Murano, and saw many churches. Venice seems to provide a seductive and relaxing total environment enfolding a person at the same time as giving one a measure of oneself. The absence of cars, buses, and trucks is more than just a release from noise, smell, and dirt. Perhaps it revives some archetypal memory of a time when man had greater control over his environment and life. The ever-present water arouses powerful images. No description of Venice would be complete without mention of its extraordinary mellow light as it reflects off the water and bathes the magnificent palaces on its canals.

Goodridge had not brought painting materials to Italy, feeling that it would be impossible to both work and see all he wanted to see in the short period of time we had at our disposal. He knew that work took over when he gave his attention to it and that he was not the type of artist to combine sketching and visiting galleries. If asked whether he would have liked to work in Venice, I suspect his response would have been similar to one he voiced in Florence as we drove in its surrounding hills. It seemed to him so man-made, so perfect, as if everything had been arranged in its rightful place, leaving nothing to be done with it by an artist. In a later interview he expressed this attitude when he said that what interested him in the Canadian landscape was its raggedness, the necessity of really seeking to construct something out of the raw materials, something that requires changing.

Piazza San Marco, Venice, 1953.

Thus it was that when we next stopped at Agay for a two-month painting stint, instead of painting the village and palm trees, he gravitated to a nearby nature reserve on the shores of the Mediterranean where the pine forest and rocks were in an untouched state. It was to some degree suggestive of Canada, despite the redness of the rocks, the blueness of the sea, the strong, bleaching light and an abandoned concrete wartime gun emplacement site.

We reached Agay indirectly, having rented a Renault in Nice and driven north in a large circle through the Alpes-Maritimes to Grenoble, then down to Avignon and Aix-en-Provence, with a brief visit to the extraordinary hill town of Les Baux. This was our first encounter with Provence, the country of so many modern French painters. For us it was a moving experience to enter their world, though I believe that seeing the landscape at Aix only increased Goodridge's sense of wonder at Cézanne's genius and left him feeling that the affinity he felt with that artist's work certainly did not reside in a shared response to that particular landscape. I imagine he felt that had he painted Mont St. Victoire he would have seen it very differently.

The perpetual sunshine and warmth, and the pleasant company

of Stanley Cosgrove and his then partner Karen in our little hotel in Agay made these two months very happy ones. It felt like a holiday, even though both Goodridge and Stanley painted almost daily. The hotel provided our meals and we ate breakfast together on the balcony, with the other two meals on the outdoor terrace. It seemed a carefree period. I was soon able to swim in the gradually warming sea and we made the occasional sortie for the day to Cannes or St. Raphael for shopping. Toward the end of our stay, Goodridge was asked to hold an exhibition at a small private gallery in St. Raphael. He had done a lot of work in Agay and was happy to be asked to exhibit it. Nothing was sold, but I do remember our amusement at the local reviewer's article because it devoted an inordinate amount of space to a description of my costume at the opening, a costume which was altogether unnoteworthy. As I remember it was just a simple summer dress.

We sailed from Southampton, which allowed us another brief stopover in London. This leave-taking from France in June of 1954 was only temporary because we planned to return to Paris in December for an exhibition planned at the Raymond Creuze Gallery. Goodridge's paintings from the year were stored in Paris until our return. When we asked the owner of the storage company for a receipt, he was verbally and visibly pained at our lack of trust in him. Goodridge was extremely embarrassed and distressed by the episode. We felt we had to insist on getting something in writing. Too much was at stake for us not to, but the situation violated someing basic in his attitude and response to people. Since we had met, Goodridge had been attempting to demonstrate that he was "business-like" and responsible, not because of any such demand on my part, but, I think, related to complaints others had made in the past. When we met, he had spoken of a trunk containing his household belongings that he had left with some friends, only to find upon our retrieving it that it was full of empty bottles and had been the one intended for the garbage. On this occasion in Paris, had I not been a witness, it is

plate 1
View of Shawanaga Bay, 1955
Oil on masonite, 80 x 120 cm

plate 2
Still Life with Leaves and Window, 1959
Oil on masonite, 72.5 x 90 cm

plate 3
Late Day, Lake Orford, 1945
Oil on canvas, 53.75 x 71.25 cm

plate 4
Reclining Nude, 1958
Oil on masonite, 90 x 150 cm

plate 5
Studio Window in Winter, 1957
Oil on masonite, 90 x 150 cm

plate 6
Charlevoix, 1950
Oil on masonite, 50 x 60 cm

plate 7
Nude on Blue Cloth, 1961
Oil on masonite, 90 x 120 cm

plate 8
Bright Day, Georgian Bay, 1962
Oil on masonite, 50 x 60 cm

more than likely that he would have left the hundred-odd paintings without a written acknowledgement from the person charged with their safe-keeping.

The first days home in Montreal were busy ones, occupied by making arrangements for our marriage, because it had now become possible. The final decree had come through before we left France, and we had had a Montreal notary draw up a marriage contract. We wanted to be married. It wrote *finis* to a long effort, and I welcomed shedding the designation of "mistress" with its illicit implication. In those days, at least in Québec, it was still difficult to find clergy willing to marry divorced couples, and the fact that we wanted to marry on the July 1 holiday in order to set off for Jacknife and Glynnis the next day, complicated the search. We just wanted to get it over with. The ceremony finally took place at the Church of All Nations on Sherbrooke at University (now the People's Church), with only our witnesses in attendance, Fred and Phyllis Poland and Basil Smith, a friend of ours. It was not to be without incident. Fred, entrusted to carry out the business side of it, had put enough bills in an envelope for the purpose. We were chagrined when the minister opened it in our presence and said, "That's not enough."

That summer we stayed at a cottage rented by friends for us while we were abroad. It was in the Laurentians, near Montfort. Our hearts sank when we saw it, because it was situated in deep woods with no view at all and no open country nearby. There was a small lake or large pond, which we named Mud Lake, but it was difficult to find any place sufficiently open to see it. For painting landscape it was surely the least promising location one could have imagined. The closed-in feeling and constant soughing of the wind in the pines towering over the cabin bothered us both, but we had paid the rent and had no alternative but to make the best of it.

We had Glynnis with us for the month of July. We felt so happy about being a little family, even though it was temporary and in a place that was far from ideal. Goodridge tried hard to look on the bright side, saying that he should be able to do something with any kind of landscape. He did find some satisfaction in trying to paint dense walls of trees, occasionally with results he felt were acceptable.

One vivid memory of that season was an event that occurred in the middle of a windy night. Those were the days when one never thought of locking up at night in a remote country cottage. We had a cat at the time that used to enter and exit by an open window over the bed. I remember being awakened by a movement of the bed-clothes and realizing that Goodridge was also awake for the same reason. Having ascertained that neither of us was responsible for whatever we had felt, we decided it must have been the cat, though in the morning when the cause of the disturbance was clear, Goodridge related how he had attempted in the night to provide an explanation for the sensation of breathing in the room not quite synchronized with his own. Discarding the possibility of it being a medical phenomenon of double breathing coming from his own lungs, he had been left with a strong feeling of a supernatural presence and fell asleep with considerable disquiet. In the morning we found a trail of burnt matches down the long path to the car along with various items strewn from my purse. The car keys, most unusually, had been left in a jacket pocket that night and so were not located by the intruder. Our reconstruction of the night's events frightened us but seemed to account for the facts. The interloper had actually touched each of us to see whether the place was occupied and by how many. As we awoke, he had frozen into silence and it was his breathing a few feet away that Goodridge had been aware of. I was rather relieved to be going into Montreal the next day to work, but the next night proved to be peaceful. A Rube Goldberg device of pails of water and clanging impediments that Goodridge rigged up in order to prevent a second silent approach was fortunately not brought into play. This minor drama had certainly taken away any little savour the cottage might have had and when our final date of departure arrived soon after, we left without any great regrets.

Goodridge and Glynnis, Montfort, Québec, summer 1954.

[top] Hanging the exhibition at the Creuze Gallery, Paris 1954.
Joan on left, unknown person on right.
[bottom] At the end of the vernissage.

We continued our preparations to return to France for the exhibition. Once again we greeted Paris at perhaps its least favourable season, arriving in early December. Our base again was the Regent's Hotel. Many details remained to be attended to for the large exhibition in the new premises of the Creuze Gallery. The plan to have it sponsored by the Canadian Embassy was conceived by Creuze himself. We were to have mixed feelings about this since we had learned from the art world that such an official sanctioning would result in critics and other *cognescenti* giving it a wide berth, producing less rather than more attention. We had done a good deal in Canada to round up and have shipped over paintings from various public collections as well as the Dominion Gallery. Max Stern resented an exhibition he had not initiated and would not control, but at least he did cooperate, albeit with predictions of failure. In the next annual contract with him he proposed a clause prohibiting Goodridge from arranging shows abroad.

With the paintings left in storage in Paris and retrieved safely, in addition to those we had brought over, there were one hundred and fifty works hung in the rather cavernous, austere, white gallery, billed as the largest private gallery in Europe. The opening arrived with more than the usual fuss because of the Embassy's involvement and Ambassador Jean Désy's presence. Also present was Gisèle Freund, the noted photographer. It had been arranged by *Weekend Magazine* in Montreal that she would take photos for a possible photo-story on the exhibition. This never materialized but a great many photos were taken.

The exhibition certainly did not take Paris by storm, but Goodridge had not expected that it would and on the whole was satisfied. There were a number of sales, all to Canadians. About ten more or less favourable reviews appeared in the press. The structure of that art world was both baffling and frustrating. It appeared that there were a few key persons whose opinion was crucial; who, if they chose to attend and were favourably impressed, would make the show an instant success by informal grapevine. This network was not accessible to us, nor did Creuze appear to wield sufficient power in the Paris gallery world to command it. Such were the problems of a non-resident Canadian attempting to break into the international art scene via Paris at that time. It was more agreeable to Goodridge, in any event, to rely on and value individual, genuine responses to the work itself than to try to manipulate power structures. Although he never made any real decision to forgo future efforts to exhibit outside Canada again, the effort, time, and money expended on this venture were never to be repeated. But for the "accident" of the Overseas Fellowship, even this one effort would not have materialized.

Shortly after our return to a more settled life in Canada, *Canadian Art* magazine (Vol. 12, no.4) asked several artists for a short statement on how the funded year abroad affected them. After thinking a great deal about it, this was what Goodridge finally submitted:

> It might be assumed that because I am a painter and because I went abroad for the purpose of looking at works of art that these works of art as such, removed from external associations, would have been what most affected me. However, I don't know that this is the case in spite of the profound pleasure I had from many of these and the conviction I felt that they were expressions of deep understanding.
>
> Perhaps rather than any revelations of a pictorial nature, I am conscious of having come to a further awareness, through my extended stay in Paris and my limited travel in a few European countries, of such wider implications as art's close identification with history, the shortness of the individual's life and the deathlessness of man's spirit. Studying as I did that year what men had briefly painted and carved during so many centuries and seeing those works in countries still disfigured and impoverished by recent

wars, had brought home to me very forcibly how this process of building up and destroying had always been going on and that in every great work of art an awareness of this need both to create and kill is evident.

In looking at these profound proofs of some men's understanding of humanity, whether through the humble jugs and loaves of Chardin, the courage and serenity of Rembrandt, Michelangelo's tormented grandeur, the joyful well-being of Renoir or the troubled fervour of Van Gogh, I felt conscious, through these men's pictures of the universality and ever-presence of such feelings and that, as there always has been, there always must continue to be this transmutation of man's spirit into forms of art.

CHAPTER TEN

Dominion Gallery

GOODRIDGE ROBERTS' association with Montreal's Dominion Gallery began in 1943, when a solo retrospective of his work was organized by Maurice Gagnon and the Gallery's owner, Rose Millman. It attracted considerable press coverage and public attention and more than half of the sixty paintings exhibited were sold.

First opened in December 1941, the gallery's collection was built upon unwanted art from the Art Association of Montreal. In 1942, Millman named Max Stern director; in 1944 they signed a partnership agreement, and in 1947, when Millman was experiencing health problems, the Gallery became the property of Max Stern and his wife Iris Westerberg.

Stern had arrived in Canada in 1941, where he was interned, first in a New Brunswick lumber camp, and then in Farnham, Québec. Originally from Dusseldorf, Germany, he was the son of a prominent art collector and owner of the Galerie Julius Stein. He received his doctorate in art history at the University of Bonn, and assumed ownership of the family art gallery after his father's death, but one year later, in 1935, he was expelled from the Reich Chamber of Fine Arts and was forced to close the gallery. He fled to England in 1937, and was interned as a civilian alien when war was declared. His position at the Dominion Gallery was obtained through the recommendation of William Birks, head of the Canadian Refugee Organization at the time. Initially, he concentrated on works of the

Old Masters, some of them from those parts of his father's collection that he had managed to take out of Germany. Then, on the advice of John Lyman and Maurice Gagnon, Stern began to concentrate on art by living Canadian artists. He signed exclusive contracts with Roberts, Lyman, Stanley Cosgrove, Jean Dallaire, and Marian Scott, an arrangement that enabled the gallery to control the market while providing some financial stability to the artists. Goodridge was the first contemporary Canadian artist exhibited under Stern's management, and the first to sign a contract with him.

Under the initial arrangement, the gallery took one-third of a painting's selling price as commission. For example, during the two years Goodridge was away in England as an Official War Artist for the Canadian Air Force, Dominion Gallery records in the Archives of the National Gallery of Canada, although sparse, show that in 1943 sixty-five works by Roberts were sold for a total of $2,417, so that the amount to which Goodridge was entitled was $1,610, and the same arrangement prevailed in 1944. During that period, as he was also receiving an officer's salary, a dealer was not crucial. In 1945 the size of Goodridge's works came under consideration when he wrote Stern that he felt his largest paintings were his best, even though they might prove more difficult to display in an exhibition. Compared to some of his later work, the largest size was only a modest 21 x 29 inches (53 x 74 cm).

Archival records do not indicate clearly when Goodridge's agreement with Stern changed from one giving the Gallery a commission on sales to one in which Stern would purchase paintings from Goodridge and give him twenty-five per cent of an agreed selling price, based on the painting's dimensions, as stated in the contract. Possibly this occurred in 1950, when Max had become sole owner of the Dominion Gallery and it opened in its new location on Sherbrooke Street West with an inaugural exhibition by Roberts. In 1948 and 1949, it was undoubtedly agreed, at least verbally, that Dominion Gallery had sole rights to Goodridge's work. Under the new contract of 1950, Stern and Goodridge agreed that Stern would guarantee purchase of enough paintings to provide Goodridge with a fixed annual income.

The agreement did not solve the financial worries that Goodridge was experiencing and that continued to haunt him over several years. His letters to Max asking for advances express his sense of being harassed by "money matters", and the need to pay off debts for income tax, dental bills, and requests from family members. In 1949 he suggested that he needed a wider market outside Canada if he were to be free of financial problems. Max, as complex a person as Goodridge himself, was facing the challenge of developing a reputation in a new country, with a new business and wife. In those early years, I believe, he and Goodridge had a liking for each other, yet they seemed also to be locked together in a kind of ritualistic dance, Goodridge complaining about his financial problems and then ending his letters with apologies and thanks to Max for all he was doing and had done for him, and Max in turn complaining about Goodridge's paintings—the colours were too dark, the subject matter too boring, vistas too short—then ending by saying that he hoped Goodridge did not mind his advice because it was well meant. Underneath their differences I believe that Goodridge had a real respect for Max's knowledge and love of art and Max in turn respected Goodridge's talent and hard-working commitment to painting. Certainly Goodridge understood what Max had experienced and lost in having to leave Germany. To my astonishment, the archives revealed that, in 1949, Goodridge proposed that Max take a commission of forty-five per cent instead of one-third "because of the great help you have been in furthering my interests." Fortunately, I don't think this suggestion was ever acted upon, as in 1948 thirty-six paintings brought him only $600, and he would surely have been hard-pressed to survive on twelve per cent less.

By the early 1950s, Goodridge's relationship with Max Stern was growing increasingly difficult. Goodridge found the annual contracts more and more irksome, since no matter how hard he worked, he could not seem to get ahead of his debts. Although exhibits featuring his work had been held at the Venice Biennale in 1952, the Carnegie International in 1952 and 1955, and the IV Centennial of Valencia, Spain, among others, this international exposure did not seem to improve Goodridge's position with Dominion Gallery. Each year involved a fresh negotiation, and Max Stern was a difficult man when it came to money matters. He continued to give Goodridge only twenty-five per cent of the selling price, while agreeing to purchase enough works sufficient to cover an annual guaranteed amount. When Goodridge and I were first together in 1952 this amount was $3,000. Three thousand dollars might have seemed a reasonable, even generous sum, but it took a great many paintings to cover it. A 12 x 16-inch (about 30 x 40 cm) oil brought us less than $25 in 1952. Under the terms of the contract, Goodridge was not to sell any of his work to other dealers, and if he sold to private persons, he could only charge Gallery prices and had to pay the Gallery ten per cent of the price.

Stern stubbornly refused to alter the basic terms of the arrangement. His response to our restiveness year by year was to increase prices by five or ten per cent, and to increase the annual guarantee, but never to pay more than twenty-five per cent of the stated selling price, even if he sold it for more. Of course this was something we could not know at the time, and only discovered on one occasion when Stern's ego got the better of him, and, expecting Goodridge to praise his salesmanship, revealed that the Beaverbrook Gallery had paid $200 above the contract price. The fact that Goodridge was painting larger works also continued to be a source of tension, because Max preferred smaller ones that were less expensive and therefore more marketable.

Every year until the end of 1956, we tried to improve the situation. We began to submit contract proposals instead of waiting to sign the one Max was offering. Max always argued that not only would Goodridge have been unknown without him, but that he was essential to Goodridge's reputation and financial security. He tried to persuade us that, without him, doom and penury would await us after the first flurry of sales had run down. He seemed oblivious to any implied oppression in the relationship, and, in fact, often made it clear that he considered his role the more important one. I think he believed it. Once, while arguing over terms, Max said that he could not engage in such prolonged discussions and reminded Goodridge that his time was more valuable than Goodridge's. Certainly he had become an important figure in Canada's art scene, and perhaps this affected his response to Goodridge in the 1950s.

A couple of small indications of Max's attitude were the book he gave us when we went abroad, *Europe on Five Dollars A Day,* and the vacuum cleaner he and his wife Iris gave us as a wedding present. We were irritated further when he reiterated the advice he continued to give to Goodridge, that he should paint snow, use brighter colours, do more smaller paintings, as well as other injunctions.

Mindful as Goodridge was of Max's importance in first obtaining some market for his work in the 1940s, it became increasingly apparent that things had changed. Many new dealers were on the scene and the market for art had expanded. Max's view was that the best strategy was scarcity: only if customers were persuaded that it was difficult to get a Roberts because their number was limited would they increase in importance, by which he meant value. A letter written by him in early 1956 says, "There should not be too many paintings on the market. It should be that people are waiting for the next picture you are creating." Valid perhaps in a market economy, but not a view that sat well with an artist who wanted maximum exposure and would have liked all those who enjoyed his work to have one. Goodridge did give a good many of his paintings away through the years, including one to a woman who admired it and cleaned for us. Twenty years later her son was forced by his circumstances to sell it to me—for $7,500.

Perhaps if Max had not been so inflexible and so determined to perpetuate a situation of vastly unequal power that felt at times like a kind of bondage, the symbiotic relationship would have continued longer. Many draft contracts were considered and revised, but the straw that broke the camel's back was a matter of a mere $200. In early 1957 Max finally offered Goodridge an annual guarantee of $7,000. The money was always paid in monthly installments and Goodridge wanted $600 a month, or $7,200. At the end of an hour's haggling neither was willing to budge. There was enough resentment stored in Goodridge to finally make him storm out of the meeting after uttering some now forgotten, uncharacteristic curse. I felt quite unprepared as to how I should deal with this kind of situation, but I managed somehow to beat a retreat while appearing calmer than I felt. I believe that the die was cast that day. Much later, after a few years had gone by, tempers had cooled, and Max seemed to have revised the whole story of the breakup in his memory, and made an effort to restore relations, but Goodridge had definitely decided to try to manage on his own.

The rupture proved to be healthy and emancipating, and Goodridge never regretted it. It meant that he was in contact with many more individual buyers and dealers who admired his painting, and this encouragement gave him increased security. The feeling of control over his life was of more than purely economic benefit. It represented independence, mastery, and competence, and these spilled over into other parts of his life. Whereas he had often been made to feel that his prolific output was undesirable, even vulgar and unseemly, he now found that it was meeting a demand from an increasing number of dealers who gave him the wider exposure he desired across the country. Paintings were consigned or sold to representatives from Winnipeg, Vancouver, Calgary, Ottawa, Edmonton, Toronto, Chicoutimi, Grand-mère, and Rouen-Noranda. Each year our income increased. In the long run, perhaps it was not beneficial for his market to have had such a large output. Every auction continues to have a goodly number of Roberts, and his prices have not risen to the same degree as those of comparable artists, but it is impossible to untangle the relationships between the art history mavens, the dealers, and other social forces who have an impact on the demand side of the market. For my part, I remain thankful for the contribution his large production has made to our family's economic well-being in the thirty-five years since his death. A great number of the paintings which have continued to be requested for exhibitions were done in the years between 1956 and 1959, including "Studio Window in Winter", "Apples and Green Cloth", "Reclining Nude", "Red Still Life", and "Still Life with Leaves and Window", to mention only a few. It was infuriating, nevertheless, to have people continually report to us that they were advised by the Dominion Gallery not to purchase anything by Roberts done after 1956 because his good work had been done before then. As I think back I wonder if this apparent antagonism sprang from Max's overweening self-confidence which truly could not credit that it was possible for good work to be produced without him.

An amusing story about Dominion Gallery concerns Rose Millman, its original owner. She had bought a painting of Marian, Goodridge's first wife, done one summer on the verandah of a rented summer cottage. It showed a clothed figure from the waist up, with a somber expression on her face. Mrs. Millman must have decided that she looked too sad or bleak to sell, so she touched it up: turned up the corners of the mouth and made the lips pink, as if the model had on lipstick. About twenty years later, we bought the painting back from Heffel Gallery in Vancouver because Goodridge liked it and wanted to return it to its original state with the help of a restorer. Abracadabra! Sure enough, there was the original mouth and lips that had been hiding for years under the layer of illicit paint. Perhaps someday, whoever owns it now will read this story of the painting's history.

CHAPTER ELEVEN

Bonnie Isle

THE SUMMER OF 1955 proved to be a high point in our life together. After the experience of Mud Lake the previous year, we were determined to find a summer place that we could count on to provide good painting material, and that would also be suitable for Glynn when she came to us for her summer holiday. Georgian Bay, especially the Pointe au Baril area that I knew and loved so well, offered the best solution. Through some now-forgotten channels we learned that an island called Bonnie Isle was available for rent. One of Georgian Bay's great assets is that the relatively sparse growth on its shorelines means that an artist can find subjects for landscape painting almost anywhere on its rocky islands. For $750 we contracted to rent Bonnie Isle for three months.

The once-extensive facilities on the island were rather dilapidated, but we did not mind since we needed only a small part for our use. The main building had several bedrooms, an immense living room with a high-built ceiling, and a huge natural stone fireplace which could accommodate a four- or five-foot log. There were also two sleeping cabins and a boathouse housing an ancient but still functioning launch and several other boats in varying degrees of disrepair. I have an old photograph, frequently reproduced, that shows Goodridge standing in front of the fireplace with a large canvas on the mantelpiece. Our power came from a generator that was supposed to provide electric light, but we seldom could figure out how to make it work, so we usually reverted to coal-oil lamps. The launch enabled us to go for our mail and supplies, although in those days a commercial boat visited twice a week to bring us ice and a grocery order. The milkman also came regularly by water.

Another feature was extra space for storage of fresh paintings. Often there were a dozen or more works in varying degrees of dryness leaning against the walls. In some places we had rented that lacked an extra room, our only alternative was to tack them onto the bare walls. This was feasible if the walls were made of wood, and even then the final honeycomb effect of small holes was not usually appreciated by most landlords.

We settled in for a long stay and Goodridge began doing water-colours, something he had not done to any extent for a number of years. Altogether he produced about sixty watercolours that season, before he went back to oils. He was full of energy and vitality and sometimes would do more than his usual routine of one painting in the morning and one in the afternoon. When the work on his water-colours went well, he could double that number easily. On rainy days when he could not work outside, he did not paint still life, but took a holiday from working. But that summer, record-breaking heat rather than rain was the predominating weather pattern. Long, frequent, and unyielding heat waves that caused much distress in the city made us grateful to be in a place where we could jump in the water and cool off with a dip whenever we wanted. Even Good-ridge, who did not much like to swim, was bathing several times a day.

As one day blended into another, Goodridge began painting oils with the same intensity and seeming effortlessness that he had finally achieved in the watercolours. Glynn's visit was a delight to us both. She overcame her fear of swimming in deep water by wearing a life-preserver, caught rock bass off the dock, hunted for frogs, played with our white poodle, picked blueberries, and gathered clam shells. We hated to contemplate the inevitable separation when the month of her visit was over. In her last week we took an overnight camping trip out to an island facing the open bay, an adventure that we recalled nostalgically in later years.

That summer Goodridge painted on a larger scale than he had ever attempted before. This was the era when a growing number of abstract artists in Canada were painting on huge surfaces. He had no inclination to do abstract work, and it often baffled him. He did not deprecate other artists' abstractions, but his own vision and motivation were inextricably linked to his need to make a statement about some kind of subject matter. He was interested, however, in doing larger works. Painting on Masonite, as he was at the time, meant that the maximum size of one dimension was four feet (122 cm). Until then, I don't think he had ever done anything larger than 36 x 48 inches (90 x 122 cm), and even this size required a complex arrangement of twine and clamps with rocks to keep the easel from overturning in the wind. The new proportions he decided to try at this time were 48 x 60 inches (122 x 152 cm). One day I prepared four boards with an undercoat of ground colour. His folding easel could not support anything that large, so for each painting he would put the board on the ground where it could be propped up by a boulder. Bent or crouched over it, he would begin to paint as speedily as possible. Despite these difficulties, these four paintings were all successful. One ended up in the National Gallery collection, one in the Beaverbrook Museum, and one in the Montreal Museum of Fine Arts. Max Stern retained the fourth in his private collection.

One day we decided to make a journey to a site overlooking open water beyond the islands. Because of our dog and the size of the board, there was no alternative but to tow a rowboat carrying the wet painting behind the launch for the return trip. This turned out to be quite an expedition; it took more than an hour each way in our antique launch. There is nothing more satisfying, though, than coming home over the water in Georgian Bay after a sun-drenched day on the rocks in the clean air.

Getting the wet painting home. Bonnie Isle, Georgian Bay, 1955.

As I write this I realize that I usually shared Goodridge's mood of either satisfaction or dejection depending on how his day's work had turned out. I always bent my energies in whatever way I could to make a contribution to his work. I prepared boards, took note of possible spots for painting, tried to create the ambience and schedule that would be most helpful, and generally tried to eliminate for him the tasks that would distract and break his concentration. He did not demand this of me, it was just part of my identification with his work and my acceptance of its importance in our life. Perhaps this role fitted well with my training to be an "enabler" in social work. I think that as time had passed I had gradually enjoyed participating in his life and sharing those responsibilities that could relieve him. For example, many young people used to write him from all over the province asking questions about his ways of working. I imagine their teachers had suggested it, but in any case I could answer these quite easily. I sometimes doubt that I would have felt the same a couple of decades later with the differing expectations of women and marriage. At the time, however, it never ceased to seem miraculous to me when the end of the day would find a new painting that had not existed in the morning. The process had for me a clear affinity with childbirth in its wondrousness. Very often I was aware of a feeling of great good fortune in being able to share this experience and to contribute to it even in a small way.

One day we saw a porcupine lumbering over the rocks. We were terrified that it might harm our dog, particularly as there was no way to get to a veterinarian. Goodridge had seen the agonies his spaniel had suffered after tackling a porcupine in the Laurentians, and he had spent hours taking out each needle with his teeth. These memories helped him to reach and accept our decision to kill this one, but neither of us felt good about it and Goodridge suffered considerable remorse both at the time and afterwards. Such an act was a violation of his natural instincts. In subsequent years, and in other places, we always managed to trap these pesky intruders and release them miles away.

Visitors that summer included the painters Fred and Nova Taylor who had recently married, a few cottagers with an interest in art who came to see the results of Goodridge's summer production and some of my relatives. Toward the end of the season Goodridge went back to doing watercolours so that there would be sufficient drying time for the oils before it was time to ship them home. He had completed about a hundred and twenty oils and sixty watercolours, making this one of the most productive summer seasons Goodridge had ever had.

CHAPTER TWELVE

The Farm

WE RETURNED to the four-room apartment on Elgin Terrace in downtown Montreal which we had rented on returning from Europe. Elgin Terrace, now supplanted by Dr. Penfield Avenue, was then a short dead-end street accessed off Peel between Sherbrooke and Pine with a small complex of attractive, brick two-storey apartments. In front were grassy terraces and the area was surrounded by lovely, grand old trees. At the end of the street was a footpath westward through the woods which led to a long wooden staircase down from Pine Avenue to Mountain Street. It was a lovely enclave of country in the centre of the city and the apartment dwellers tended to be neighbourly and companionable. We frequently walked this way to visit friends. When we had first moved in after returning from France, the four rooms with one of its two bedrooms serving as studio space had seemed a vast improvement over our earlier two rooms with kitchenette on Pine Avenue. Now again, we were aware of insufficient space and with some improvement in our financial situation, felt that we could afford to look for a larger place.

In May of 1956 we rented the second and third floors of a terraced Victorian row house on Grosvenor Avenue, just above Sherbrooke Street in Westmount. The ceilings were high, there were four rooms upstairs, a back shed, and an old deck off the kitchen. In its slightly shabby way it had considerable charm and to us it seemed like a real home. The front rooms on both levels had large bay windows. The spacious master bedroom became the studio and another bedroom was used to store paintings. The unheated shed held trunks, crates, and other miscellany. But we were often reminded that this was not our own house by the angry pounding from the ground floor when we were nailing up a crate to ship out paintings.

Another unexpected development in our living arrangements brought an important change in both Goodridge's work life and in our life generally. In the autumn of 1955, we were asked by Ghitta Caiserman and Alfred Pinsky whether we wanted to look at a farm property about 65 miles (100 km) from Montreal near Calumet, which was for sale and which they could not afford to buy alone. We made the trip one weekend and felt it had much to recommend it: hilly country with some open fields, a small stream running through it, an old log house, barn, and outbuildings, with about 85 acres (34 hectares) of property.

On the financial side, a half-share would cost us $2,000. At the rate of cottage rental, four summers there would more than cover it and we could walk away without a loss. What we did not consider was the attachment we would develop, the improvements we would want to make, and the many subtle ties that bound Goodridge, myself, Glynnis—and later Tim—to the place until many years after Goodridge's death.

It was our refuge from the city at all seasons, a restorative place where it was so much easier to feel peaceful, close to nature, in touch with both the earth and the sky. We put in a large vegetable garden and got pleasure from planting, weeding, mulching, harvesting, and eating the produce at the end of the process. Dwarf apple trees had been put in by the previous owner and each year we were happy to make loads of applesauce from the windfalls and the rather wormy apples that stayed on the tree until they were ripe. It became a ritual, performed mostly by Glynnis and myself, to plant all but the least hardy crops on the long weekend in May, trying at the same time to outwit the hordes of black flies when there was no wind.

We divided the buildings on the property as equitably as possible. We took the original farmhouse which had three rooms on the ground floor and an open attic. Alfie had the little house that the previous owner had built to provide shelter should the farmhouse burn down in the winter. Alfie also had the henhouse and most of the large barn. The couple separated the winter of our purchase, so that Ghitta never did come, and Alfie did not come back until 1960 with his second wife Claire Hogenkamp, a sculptor. Claire loved birds and cats as well! Soon the property had many little birdhouses nailed to the fence posts to provide nesting places for the bluebirds which were in profusion in the fifties. She was also a godsend to me in looking after Tim in later days. Somewhat surprisingly, all four of us found that we enjoyed getting together quite often in the evenings and playing solitaire. With four sets of aces to use, play became raucous and hilarious fun.

By the summer of 1956 we had moved in for the season. Our living arrangements were fairly simple, but they were livable. There was electricity, an outhouse, and gravity-fed running cold water from a spring a quarter mile away. We managed to acquire a bare minimum of second-hand furniture and settled into the joys and tribulations of being property owners. It gave Goodridge the sense of being a solid citizen of sorts. The attic opened up the possibility of painting still life on wet or cold days. Now that he was no longer teaching, we were able to move out in late April and stay through the early fall. My job, first as a psychiatric social worker at the Allan Memorial Institute and then as a fieldwork supervisor at the McGill School of Social Work, enabled me to have three months off in the summer due in part to my exceptionally enlightened bosses.

What had always been a sharp and often difficult transition for Goodridge between painting landscape in the summer and still life and figures in the winter became more blurred and a great many fine still lifes were done there in the late fifties and early sixties. Abundant blossoms and wildflowers meant he could always find

[top] The farmhouse near Calumet, Québec, summer 1956.
[bottom] Jim Borcoman, Tim, Thérèse Borcoman, Alfred Pinsky, 1964.

[top] Joan and Goodridge with Bill Kinnis at the farm, 1957.
[bottom] With Glynnis and the dogs, 1958.

subjects, and he now had no problem in finding the space to work and to store wet paintings. For the first time he tried painting autumn colours, something he had always avoided as long as Stern was urging him to do so. Now that he was no longer under contract to Stern, this was no longer relevant. He had always felt the colours were too garish and never really became totally comfortable with painting during those weeks when the colours were strongest. Nevertheless he was always pleased when the work was successful.

A little stream ran through the property and a primitive dam we had built provided us with a small swimming hole that first summer. Unfortunately it did not survive and its replacement with concrete that Alfie put in was also unable to withstand the spring runoff. In the winters, the cross-country skiing was excellent as there were many old logging roads and fine paths made by the cows which local farmers allowed to roam unfenced. One spring we watched the amazing sight of a calf being born practically on our doorstep. We came up in the late fall to cut a small spruce for our Christmas tree, and on several occasions celebrated either Christmas or New Year's there, glorying in the old-time ways of such country celebrations.

There were a couple of exhibits in Québec City. On one occasion we were invited with our mutual friends Bob and Helen Duffy to have dinner at the home of Jean-Paul and Madeleine Lemieux. Glistening glassware and white linen were making me feel a bit of a country bumpkin but that was as nothing compared to the discomfort we felt when Helen, inadvertently, but with a grand gesture of her arm, upset her full glass of red wine over the pristine white tablecloth. Madeleine was distressed but gracious as we tried to mop it up, dilute it with salt, and carry on as if nothing had occurred. Jean-Paul acted as if it were an everyday occurrence.

During the summers between 1956 and 1959 we made a few short trips to other parts of the country. In 1957, we took a brief boat trip up the St. Lawrence to Tadoussac and spent several days in Baie St. Paul with the painter Bill Kinnis and his wife Gladys. In 1958 we drove to Cape Breton and spent a couple of weeks there. In 1959 two or three weeks were spent at Pointe au Baril on Georgian Bay. These trips and others later were conceived primarily to add variety to my daughter's annual visits.

Goodridge did paint in Cape Breton and found the landscape challenging. Unfortunately, though, there was not enough time to really settle into it and develop a close identification with that part of the country. Generally he found that good painting always required him to be in one locality for a period of time, unless he had already spent time there on another occasion, as was the case with Georgian Bay. He could not be a peripatetic artist in the manner of A. Y. Jackson with his many, varied sketching trips. Probably this was because it nearly always took him at least a week to get rolling. He has recorded that each summer season he felt as if he had to relearn how to paint landscape again. In a sense this relearning was also required in new settings. To me it seemed less like relearning than developing a connection with his surroundings. He described to me spending two weeks in the Gatineau one summer in the 1930s, not painting at all at first because nothing seemed to stimulate him. At the end of a couple of weeks some little piece of the country moved him to try a watercolour and after that he continued working feverishly on one after another.

We still retained our connection with Georgian Bay, as we had to pick up Glynnis there each year and return her after a month. We usually broke the journey by spending some days or weeks at Wawonaissa, my sister Mary Ortved's island at Pointe au Baril. In preparation for a longer stay there in 1959, we had a carpenter build us two plywood boxes with slots on three surfaces that would safely accommodate a dozen or more freshly painted Masonite boards for the journey home. This took care of the smaller-sized paintings; another box was constructed to hold a dozen canvases, 25 x 32 inches (64 x 81 cm). The flexibility of Masonite made it impossible to use the slotted-box model for such a size. This explains Goodridge's occasional

[top] Goodridge painting, Calumet, Québec, 1959.
Photo by Albert de Niverville.
[bottom] Displaying new paintings in front of the farmhouse, 1959.

return to canvas in the late '50s after having painted exclusively on Masonite for a good many years. Although the surface used perhaps had aesthetic consequences, as has been suggested by some writers, the initial choice of Masonite was also for practical reasons. Both economy and the fact that a far greater number could be stacked in a limited space played a role in the choice. In the first years when he used only a transparent rabbit skin glue for a base, he commented on his satisfaction in building light up out of the dark ground. Later he seemed to prefer coating the board with a white primer.

In the winter of 1959, Goodridge decided that we were throwing money away by continuing to pay rent and that we should buy a house. An advertisement for a house on Lansdowne Avenue backing onto Westmount Park caught our eye. We went to see it and decided to buy it without looking at much else, primarily because of its location on the park with its grass, walkways, and beautiful trees. We had some anxious afterthoughts, wondering whether we could sustain the responsibility of two mortgages on it without any assured income. Before we took possession on May 1, however, the University of New Brunswick asked Goodridge to be their first resident artist, beginning in September. The mortgages would be covered.

CHAPTER THIRTEEN

Fredericton

IN EARLY SEPTEMBER 1959, after Goodridge had accepted the New Brunswick offer and I had obtained a leave of absence from my work with McGill social work students, we set off from Calumet to Fredericton. We had succeeded in renting our newly-acquired but as yet unlived-in house. The station wagon was loaded with our belongings and our two poodles. Paintings had been crated and shipped off by rail. We had a rented house to go to, thanks to the thoughtfulness of those responsible in Fredericton, and instructions about where to get the key, but the street or location meant nothing. When Goodridge had last lived there in 1929 with the threat of poverty omnipresent in his chosen field, he had resolved not to return until he had amassed $50,000. He would tell this story, like many he told about himself, with wry amusement and utter detachment, as if it were about someone else. As it turned out, Goodridge had not amassed anything to speak of and we quite happily lived month to month.

We set out with a high sense of adventure and excitement. The past was temporarily in storage with the furniture, and the coming year was an unknown quantity. This was the first work with a regular full-time salary that Goodridge had had since returning from France six years earlier. The fixed demands of the university's invitation seemed extraordinarily light: three lectures and the mounting of an exhibition.

As the long miles passed, we listened to the car radio which reported with barely concealed shock that Krushchev had taken off his shoe in the United Nations and banged it on the desk in fury. It seemed as though the world might be on the brink of another war. We were upset at what this U.N. event might portend, but when we arrived in Fredericton, we found it of less than passing interest to those we met. It was the first of numerous occasions in which we felt a kind of isolation from the rest of the world. At first we felt a sense of frustration at the importance given to local affairs that intensified our feeling that we were outsiders, but gradually our sense of alienation diminished as we became more a part of the community, made friends, and bit by bit came to enjoy the insulation ourselves. The sense of peace induced by the absence of complexity and remoteness from turbulent world events now seemed a rare asset.

Lucy Jarvis, director of the Art Centre, was a key person throughout the year. I believe she had been instrumental in conceiving the idea of a resident artist for the university, in developing committee support, and then that of Colin Mackay, the president. I am sure she also played a major role in suggesting that Goodridge be the first incumbent. She continued to give him her support and encouragement in a myriad ways throughout the year.

My memories of that year are of beautiful fall days—once we had settled in and become more or less resigned to the deep pink walls in our house—when we explored the countryside and Goodridge spent many hours painting outdoors. Jim Bedell and his wife were delighted to let him paint from their farm overlooking the St. John River on Keswick Ridge. The leaves were splendid in their fiery colours, the sky and water a limpid blue. I remember three large paintings done from there, one of which was later given to the university. The warm, friendly visits we spent with the Bedells were an important part of those days of initiation, and we found we shared many of their social and political concerns.

Autumn gave way to winter and snow which never seemed to stop falling. Shovelling the driveway and walk became a part of our daily routine, as it had never been in Montreal. The weather did not seem to discourage the people in Fredericton and events at the Art Centre were well attended despite raging blizzards. The Centre, built originally as a temporary wartime hut, was a central focus in our Fredericton life. On Friday evenings, any who wished could draw from a live model. A philosophy professor gave an aesthetics class there. Poetry readings, seminars, lectures, exhibitions, and sometimes just a simple supper and pleasant conversation were held in that building. Since indoor painting was almost impossible in our limited quarters, Lucy negotiated studio space in the nursing department next to the Art Centre and Goodridge managed to do a bit of still-life painting there.

The forthcoming exhibition, a requirement of the resident artist post, was an incentive to try to maintain a regular work schedule despite the distractions. Goodridge was not used to being a minor celebrity and was often, if not always, uncomfortable with the role. On the whole, his retiring disposition preferred anonymity because he was always conscious of what he considered his frailties, and renown and deference tended to highlight these for him. This was perhaps a part of what is often cited as his humility and modesty. The other side of the coin was a kind of unfailing conviction in his work and his potential as an artist even when he was unsatisfied with a particular work. Always he was both pleased and relieved when people whom he liked admired a painting. These feelings of having been given an extraordinary gift just short of realization are beautifully described in his own writing. There were times when his potential as an artist and he himself as a person were fully integrated into an impressive confidence and conviction. At other times his person felt to him more like a channel through which something he could not understand was being acted out.

Much of my time was spent taking French conversation lessons with Thérèse Borcoman. This was the beginning of an enduring association with Thérèse and Jim. They later moved to Ottawa and

Jim was a key participant in organizing the National Gallery's Roberts Retrospective in 1969-70.

Many others, too, took us into their lives. Frank and Norah Toole, Vi and Rosie Rosenberg, the Paceys, the Hales, were all faculty members who had a keen interest in the arts and befriended us along with Nan Gregg in the library and Madge Smith with her bookstore/ art gallery in town. In fact, the hospitality and kindness of the people of Fredericton made the ten months unforgettable. Towards the end when Goodridge was asked to remain another year, the prospect became close to a real temptation and we thought about it very carefully. Had we not just bought the house in Montreal and had it not been so far away from Glynnis, we might easily have succumbed. In later, unhappier years, we sometimes wondered what our life would have been like had we stayed.

On days when it was not too bitterly cold, Goodridge started to paint some winter landscapes from the car. The procedure was necessarily awkward in the front seat and he had to confine himself to small sizes. He had never before painted landscapes in the winter despite repeated urgings by Max Stern. In fact it was a kind of point of honour not to yield to something Max considered commercial, and it was just the sort of advice that brought out his stubborn independence. Now that Stern had ceased to play a part in marketing his work, it was possible to explore this new subject matter.

A large window in our home overlooking the slope down to the St. John River was the subject of a very fine landscape, owned for a time by Stanley Cosgrove. The first signs of spring and the ice breakup on the river brought Goodridge other exciting possibilities. We would drive out of town downriver to find accessible sites that drew his attention. On mild, sunny days it was possible to work outside the car and in a larger format.

Spring also brought the required exhibition closer. Our assumption had always been that it would be held in the new Beaverbrook Art Gallery, the only adequate exhibition space in town. Our opinion was shared by others including, I believe, Colin Mackay, the president, but it became clear that this had not been pre-arranged and it seemed that only Lord Beaverbrook himself could authorize such an unusual event. Suddenly we had an insight into the complex power relations of the town as efforts got underway to bring about a resolution to our problem. Goodridge was dismayed at the snags and felt it would be in the nature of an intolerable insult were he refused space in the Gallery. No doubt this issue was exacerbated by feelings he had almost forgotten of neglect from the Fredericton community as a young artist many years earlier. In any case, word filtered up the line that he would not exhibit except in the Beaverbrook Gallery, which created pressure on the university to save face. Finally the authorization came through and the confrontation was averted.

Preparations accelerated. We bought moulding, a mitre box, saw and nails and began making several dozen frames on our living room floor. Paintings were sent in from Toronto where they had been on consignment, to add to those we had brought and those painted while in Fredericton. Goodridge felt he wanted to be represented by more than just a few months' work, although on the whole he felt moderate satisfaction in what he had accomplished in this period, considering that there had been more than the usual number of distractions.

The exhibition proved successful and Frederictonians seemed happy and proud of their "native son".

Augmenting the usual tension of holding an exhibition was the news that Goodridge had been selected by the University of New Brunswick Senate to receive an honorary LL.D. in May. This was an extremely significant event for Goodridge. He was riven by complex and contradictory feelings about his family and New Brunswick, the two being closely joined emotionally. Independence and the need to succeed on his own terms and in his own chosen field of painting were mixed with a combination of pride in his work and self-doubt

Goodridge receiving an honorary degree from Colin Mackay, president of the University of New Brunswick, May 1960.

when he compared the achievements of family members to his own. So many of them had accomplished so much in literature in the first half of the twentieth century that the bar seemed to have been set very high for him. It is unfortunate that he never saw the letter, now in the University of New Brunswick archives, that Charles G. D. Roberts wrote to his daughter Edith, saying that he believed she would live to see Goodridge acclaimed as the genius of the family. Being honoured with the degree meant recognition by New Brunswick as one of theirs who had matched the achievements of all the other members of his family, and a vindication of his choice of painting as a career. The convocation itself was a pageant of colour with the brilliant hoods in procession on the fresh spring grass of the campus, vividly green in the sunlight. I found it impressive and quite moving.

Dorothy Roberts Leisner, Goodridge's older sister, was invited from Pennsylvania to give a poetry reading just prior to convocation, and spent a few days with us. One night there was a severe thunderstorm with much lightning and booming claps of thunder overhead. Dorothy became very anxious and distraught and Goodridge reprimanded her in a critical, angry way. The argument spilled over into other matters and I remember trying to smooth over the situation while being shocked at Goodridge's uncharacteristic unkindness. It seemed further evidence that the convocation was bringing out early family conflicts and rivalries. He could not stand her rather unkempt appearance and old-fashioned clothing, something that certainly would have been no cause for concern in anyone else. They both seemed to get over their rancour once Fredericton was left behind.

Several trips to other parts of the province were an important part of our memories and experiences of the year. We went to Moncton to visit Goodridge's mother and aunts, to Sussex to visit the potters Kjeld and Erika Deichmann, where we saw his impressive pottery in the beautiful setting in which they lived, and to St. John for a visit with Jack and Jean Humphrey. Goodridge had known Jack since the 1930s but had not seen him for a long time. Visits with other artists always had a different quality, even if they were mainly social, from social contacts with all but the closest friends. I am sure this arose from a shared relationship to life and outside reality, no matter how much their work or their circumstances differed from Goodridge's. Much could be taken for granted and some sort of basic understanding was created from the start.

One of the required lectures Goodridge was scheduled to give was to be held at the Mount Allison University School of Fine Art. These lectures were one of the big distractions from his painting in this year because speaking in public did not come easily for Goodridge. He would usually spend many days trying to write something, uncertain whether to read a formally prepared text or talk off-the-cuff, trying to define a topic and to find something worthwhile to say about it. His reluctance regarding public speaking was complicated by the fact that he found most writing on art pretentious, boring, obvious, or irrelevant. He had little interest in theories of art. He used to tell the story of a young child asking his older brother what the balloons with words in a comic strip were. The older one replies, "Those are for the people who can't understand the pictures." To him, art books were useful for their reproductions. Consequently, when called upon to give a talk, he would often discard material on which he had spent considerable time and effort, and decide that the only subject on which he was an authority was his own work. On the Mount Allison occasion, he planned to illustrate his lecture with slides I had taken of work he had done the previous summer.

Slide technology, at least to us, was in its infancy and we had purchased a hand projector which would show two different sizes of slides. For some reason we mounted each of them between two sheets of glass which were taped together with black electric tape. The outcome in Sackville was disastrously amateurish, if amusing. I manipulated the machine while Goodridge talked. Too long an interval between changes produced melted tape and a jammed slide which required disgorging the innards of the projector to release. In addition, the quality of the colours left much to be desired, but our hosts (including Lawren Harris, Jr.) were generous in their reception and response.

That trip included a visit with Alex Colville and his wife. In 1955 Goodridge had received a warm and positive letter from Alex Colville, whom he had never met, occasioned by his having seen an exhibition which Max Stern had circulated in the Maritimes. This unsolicited appreciation from one whose own work was so different typified Alex's generous nature and made us both eager to make his acquaintance.

We enjoyed them and their beautiful home and I remember how interesting I found their conversation. Alex's analytic intelligence and broad interests seemed different from other painters I had met. From that meeting a curious memory remains. They wanted to renovate their kitchen, but had refrained because they

Grand Manan, May 1961.

did not want to alter or interfere with their children's memories of how things had been placed as they grew up. I think this memory stayed with me because Glynnis had experienced so much change and I had never given much importance to physical change in my preoccupation with emotional shifts; nor in the larger demands of parenting and living could I imagine paying attention to what I considered to be minor matters. Except for one further visit in 1961 during a summer trip to Grand Manan, our friendship with the Colvilles was unfortunately not renewed after our departure from Fredericton.

We were invited to spend the long weekend in May with our friends Frank and Norah Toole at their summer home on the island of Grand Manan in the Bay of Fundy. We had come to enjoy their company immensely, their informal, easygoing, yet understanding warmth. As well as his eminence as a scholar and chemist, Frank's deeply aesthetic sensibility found expression in his love of music and in his personality. He seemed to understand and appreciate Goodridge from some shared place. As a result, Goodridge's wit and humour flowered in his presence. His memory for amusing anecdotes sharpened with Norah and Frank's response, and stories tumbled out one after another. The Grand Manan visit was a great antidote to the tensions of the exhibition behind us, and the island itself with its cliffs and gentle shores captured our hearts as well. We returned the following summer to stay a couple of weeks and Goodridge painted a bit though the time was too brief to do much.

Before we left, May and early June brought the opportunity to do a number of paintings near Kingsclear or Springhill where the St. John River is divided into numerous channels by islands with their hay barns. It was in the same general area that Goodridge remembered spending one summer as a boy in a cottage with his family. His father had done a mural on one of the walls of the birds and animals of the region—the only time he could recall his father demonstrating any ability as a painter. On this occasion the owner had indicated we would be welcome to use his property, which was on a hill with a fine view of the islands. Goodridge must have gone more than once as I recall at least four paintings done there. One was bought by then-Premier Richard Hatfield and later donated to the Beaverbrook Gallery. Another was used to pay my surgeon for an operation a few years later, still in pre-medicare days. It was the last spate of work done before we returned to Québec. Leaving Fredericton meant leaving behind much we hated to part from, but this was accompanied by our feeling that the warm attachments we had made would surely be followed up in some way in the future.

CHAPTER FOURTEEN

Back Home

THE SIGHT THAT GREETED US on our return to the farm was horrendous. Our neighbour had been using our barn to store feed for his sheep, but had sold them off the previous autumn. When the last kernels of grain had been consumed, the rats had abandoned the barn and come into the house in a desperate search for food during the winter. The result was total chaos. Everything on the open kitchen shelves had been toppled and the contents consumed where possible. The bookcases had been attacked and the book spines chewed for the glue in them. Excrement and filth were everywhere. A rude homecoming after a long drive. Despite our fatigue, hours of cleaning were required before we could think of spending the night. Finally we were able to go to bed. Rat poison in the basement took care of the laggards in subsequent days.

Two rented nags provided entertainment for Glynnis and her friend Ann during July at the farm. Our fears that they would run away with the girls proved quite unfounded. In fact the reverse was the case; they would often not move at all without huge encouragement and prodding. One even had to be exchanged, but the girls had great pleasure in looking after them and I think they learned a good deal about the care and feeding of horses.

We spent a month at Pointe au Baril and then were able to take possession of our new house in Montreal. Almost immediately Goodridge decided to add a studio onto the rear of the house. With the architectural help of Max Roth and Joe Baker, the addition was completed by the summer of 1961 and Goodridge was able to move his equipment from the master bedroom into larger and brighter space. One wall facing northeast was completely glass. It was the first actual studio he had ever had. Not surprisingly perhaps, such a flawless space added a certain amount of pressure. There was no excuse not to turn out flawless paintings. Fortunately familiarity took care of this problem before long. He came to enjoy the large space where he could have models and do large still lifes more easily than on Grosvenor. He always found it more of a chore to have to find a model and then be ready at the appointed time than to buy a bouquet of flowers and some fruit. Another dilemma related to working from a model was the question of conversation. Goodridge did not want it for himself, but was conscious that the model might not relish hour after hour of total silence. Together with the cost, these things probably explain why he did fewer figures than still lifes. They were equally unmarketable until the last few decades when suddenly still life became much more desired than landscape, and market prices reflect this today. I was frequently pressed into service as a model, but unless I could read at the same time, I found it unbearably boring as well as strangely exhausting. He did do a very fine series of "golden nudes" in 1961 and 1962 with Hélène Ouvrard, whom he felt very comfortable with, as a model.

The peace activist group Voice of Women was a strong organization in the early 1960s. I belonged to a chapter that was trying to raise money for a group called the Peace Research Institute, made up of a few social and physical scientists, headed by Dr. Norman Alcock, who felt research on the causes of war was a means by which peace in the world could be achieved. A much-used fundraising device of those days was an art auction where artists donated a portion of the sale price at a sale or auction run by the fundraising organization. Our chapter put one on at the Windsor Hotel and Betty MacNeill and I undertook co-chair responsibilities. We enlisted a great number of the professional artists of that day, both French- and English-speaking, and I don't remember any artist refusing to exhibit. It was a tremendous amount of work but we did well in sales and I think netted some $7,000 for the cause. Needless to say, peace was not achieved and such naïve, idealistic views seem far away in today's warring world.

We returned briefly to Grand Manan in 1961 and then again spent a month at the same rented cottage we had had the year before at Pointe au Baril. It was out toward the open water with only a few small cedar trees to break the exposure to the prevailing west wind. On this rather barren island with the wind, the whitecaps on the water and the dazzling sunshine, Goodridge's output became increasingly expressionistic. In these years he was also looking at reproductions of Emil Nolde and others of the German expressionist school of painters.

CHAPTER FIFTEEN

A New Arrival

WE HAD BOTH WANTED to have children from our very first days together. I think I had always envisaged a family with at least four children as being desirable. When I did not get pregnant, we consulted a gynecologist who did fertility work, and abortions on occasion, and was sympathetic to all in need of his services. The diagnostic requirements proved to be very unwelcome, an appointment for both of us at a specific time preceded by intercourse an hour before. I think it was to see if the sperm had swum far enough upstream or something of that nature. It felt mechanical and destructive of the relationship and there seemed no sure treatment for tired, reluctant sperm so we abandoned it in frustration and depression and decided to explore adoption.

The Montreal agency for those who were neither Jewish nor Roman Catholic was the Children's Service Centre, and they concluded that we were too old, I thought. We next tried the appropriate agency in Burlington, Vermont, but they too rejected us. A neurologist I had come to know while working at the Neuro offered artificial insemination to me. I knew no one who had gone that route and decided against it, not only because he would not tell me where he would procure the sperm and so I imagined it would have been his own, but also because I could not imagine how a child would be able to deal with having an unknown father or how, in fact, I could handle it.

A sociologist at McGill, an expert in the field of adoption and father of several adopted children, put us in touch with a woman in California who was seeking adoptive parents for her coming baby. It would cost us $1,200 and there seemed a lot of complications, but before that scenario was played out we were stunned to receive a telephone call in the early autumn of 1962 from the Children's Service Centre in Montreal saying that if we were willing to consider a baby with some aboriginal ancestry, there was a baby boy for us in Nova Scotia, only a few weeks old. We leapt at the news and went out to buy a crib. It felt strange to be anticipating a baby without an eight- or nine-month lead time.

Meanwhile, Goodridge had already done a tremendous amount of painting in 1962. He had had the experience of working on the riverbank of the St. John River as spring breakup began and he decided to do the same thing on the Gatineau River north of Ottawa. Sometimes he worked from inside the car on a small scale but when the sun shone and it was agreeably warm, he would set up his folding easel outside. He spent about three weeks in March and early April in Wakefield, living in the local hotel, where I joined him on the weekends. It was a good start to what proved to be a long, productive season. May and June were spent at the farm in Calumet doing landscapes and still lifes.

While Glynnis and her friend Ann Percival, a daughter of my old friends Kay and Ed, were with us in July, we had rented the summer home of Dr. Max Dunbar, the McGill biologist and former thesis supervisor of my brother John. The house was located in the Eastern Townships on a high ridge above Lake Massawippi with incredible views of the surrounding countryside and mountains. A green expanse stretched out before one's eyes whether looking from the front or the back. Glynnis and Ann were busy catching butterflies that month while Goodridge painted large boards where the vistas dominated. Some days we drove down to the lake for a swim and a change of pace. The spare bedroom was filling up rapidly with large works when the month ended.

Once again we spent a couple of weeks with my sister at Pointe au Baril during August and came to the decision to search for an island of our own. The Ontario Department of Lands and Forests in Parry Sound supplied us with a long list of all the islands in the Pointe au Baril area of three acres (1.2 hectares) or less, the maximum allowed for a single purchase. Armed with maps and an outboard motorboat, we visited them. Many were not much more than large shoals with only the scrubbiest of vegetation, no elevation and no trees to speak of. Finally we found one that had just what we were searching for. It was amoeba-shaped, two and a half acres (one hectare), with one end on high ground looking down Shawanaga Bay and the other end lower and facing a sizable island, also unoccupied and Crown Land. The back of the island was very close in one part to a huge island which had a deep bay in its shoreline. This area too was Crown land and when further sales of Crown Land were frozen in 1963, it guaranteed us complete privacy and a good measure of isolation for the foreseeable future. On our island-to-be were many mature white pines, some cedars near the water's edge, even blueberry bushes, altogether a most felicitous location which we were most fortunate and happy to have found.

We applied for a patent which required that a survey be done and a building erected with a value of at least $1,200, if my memory is accurate. Property costs were $300 per acre. The purchase of a prefabricated Pan Abode cottage made of western red cedar logs seemed to be the best plan. In those days it was shipped by rail from B.C. in a boxcar which was then unloaded on a siding at the C.P.R. railway station in Pointe au Baril for the builder to truck down to the water. There it was loaded onto a barge and towed to the building site some nine miles away. Modest as the cottage was, when it was finally erected it was going to be significantly above the $1,200 minimum required, but we concluded it was financially possible and found a contractor who promised to complete the task by the next summer.

Goodridge and Tim, 1964.

In Montreal as the time drew near for our new baby to come to us, we learned that he had fallen ill with pneumonia in his temporary foster home and could not leave until he was well. To feel that our son was being cared for without our participation was strangely painful even though we had never seen him. They could not possibly be doing the right things, we felt. After a few weeks, though, we were able to fly to Sydney and bring him home. We chose Timothy as his first name and Gostwick, a Roberts family name from England, as his middle name. He was eleven weeks old, quite adorable, with a head of straight black hair, more copious than I had ever seen before in a baby. My anxiety was low, having done it all before. Goodridge rather quickly became comfortable with sharing early morning or late night feedings, and growing attached to the little helpless creature that all babies are.

He also became involved in doing a series of very small oil still lifes on 4 x 6-inch (10 x 15 cm) wooden panels which he had bought in Paris but never used. Altogether there were about twenty-five of these jewel-like miniatures, and when the panels were exhausted, he tried some on 8 x 10-inch (20 x 25 cm) Masonite boards. It was a very long and successful season, more than seven months of almost continuous work. In retrospect I think he must have been totally exhausted and mentally drained. Nevertheless, at the end of 1962 we felt very blessed and happy. We had no premonitions about the future.

CHAPTER 16

The Final Years

IN EARLY 1963, all our good fortune seemed to evaporate. Events intruded that were outside our control. I was found to have a nodule on my thyroid gland and the doctors recommended that I have it removed lest it become malignant. I was told I would have to be in the hospital for a week or ten days. The prospect of looking after the baby all by himself made Goodridge so uneasy that we hired a housekeeper for the period. Everything went well, except that I was now required to take thyroid pills for the rest of my life and they do not seem to adjust as readily as when the body's gland takes care of that function.

It was not long before the Front de Libération du Québec put a bomb in a mailbox in Westmount, which resulted in a soldier's severe injury. This accentuated the climate of menace that was starting to permeate the Anglo milieu in Montreal. Goodridge seemed particularly affected by this event. He abhorred violence, but also was very self-conscious about his difficulty in using the French language. Actually his respect for language in general inhibited him from using it imperfectly. Perhaps for these reasons, perhaps for others such as the titanium and lead in paint, and perhaps for none of them, his anxiety and agitation grew and soon produced a complete nervous and physical collapse. I was quite frantic. I called our family doctor, who saw him immediately and arranged admission to the Allan Memorial Institute that same day for treatment of depression. The doctors were extremely positive about his prognosis, saying that his recovery would be rapid and complete. And so we went off to the farm not long after his discharge. I remember clearly our discussion about whether he felt able to drive, whether any instructions had been given by his doctor about whether he should drive (they had not) and my worry about what stance I should adopt. By the end of July he decided that we should go to the island where our new cottage awaited us. A bed, a card table and four chairs, a crib and other bare essentials had been ordered from Eaton's catalogue and they were to be in place for our arrival. En route we spent the night at the local hotel in Killaloe, where they were willing to let us have our poodles in the room. The trip, though long in those days, taking about an hour just to get from one end of Ottawa to the other, was relatively painless because we did not know then about car seats for children and Tim played with the dogs and his toys, even napped briefly, in the back of our station wagon. On our boat trip to the island, we stopped at my sister's island to announce our presence in the area. Mary told us about the unusual number of rattlesnakes on the islands that year. This news, combined with baby Tim's new ability to crawl, was sufficient to bring on an acute recurrence of Goodridge's fears and worries. We landed, unpacked and settled in, but our stay was brief. After only one night it became apparent to me that I could not handle the situation with a baby and a very sick husband, alone on an island nine miles by boat from the mainland and any medical help. Fortunately, Mary's husband Bill was a doctor and he agreed that we should return to the city. They helped me to close up the cottage and we drove with Goodridge to Toronto. There we left our car, and also Tim, with kind friends. We flew to Montreal where Goodridge was rapidly rehospitalized for a longer period. It was a melancholy end to our hopes for a return to normalcy for that summer.

In 1964 Goodridge's progress toward rehabilitation was once again put on hold when I had to again enter hospital to have a hysterectomy. It was as if the fates were really conspiring against us.

We were not able to do anything much for the summer of 1964. It seemed to be a losing struggle for Goodridge to try and regain his former health. Hope alternated with deep despair for me as I tried to live with his continuing agonizing misery and agitation, at the same time trying to protect Tim from their impact. Friends were helpful and we had a paid live-in housekeeping service once again. I remember how complicated and detailed my written instructions had to be for Tim's food and daily schedule. I was so afraid he would suffer from my absence.

All the psychiatric profession had to offer Goodridge at the time were early drugs and electroshock. The drugs had many very debilitating side effects. One that I remember resulted in an inability to urinate and a consequent toxic psychosis for which he had to be transferred from the Douglas to the Royal Victoria Hospital for an operation. He developed pernicious anaemia and needed a nurse to give him injections of vitamin B12 every month. The many shock treatments he had through the years (probably close to a hundred) produced not only the so-called temporary memory loss but also a profound sense of being violated in his innermost being. At times it seemed as if he might emerge from the grip of his unending fears, but always the extreme agitation returned and hospitalization was again recommended when he worsened and I could no longer endure it at home. There was no such thing as respite care in those days. It was the agitation that I found so intolerable, minute by minute and day after day. Over the years I experienced a continuous, gradual loss of hope for anything better in the future. Hospital was anathema for such a private man, but by 1974 he had had seven admissions. I don't believe the doctors had any real idea of why he had become so ill. Now it might be possible to explore whether lead poisoning from his paint was involved or any other toxic *sequelae*. Medical understanding of severe depression is greater now, but then it was, it seemed, just put down to his lifelong depressive personality. At such times one searches interminably for an explanation, an understanding of

Glynnis, Goodridge, and Tim in Westmount Park, August 1965.

the "why." Although he had never mentioned any possible connection of his depression to the changes going on in the art world and the swing away from figuration and *art vivant*, I could not help wondering, almost clandestinely, in later years whether he unconsciously had felt a premonition of his possible irrelevance and an inability to respond to it.

By the summer of 1965 his condition was somewhat improved and in an attempt to get back to normality, we rented a farmhouse near Knowlton for a month where he worked quite steadily. The weather was quixotic that month with many severe thunderstorms. One time while Alf Pinsky and his wife Claire were with us for the weekend a storm erupted and a ball of fire was actually visible in the kitchen for a few seconds bouncing along the floor. No one mentioned it in order not to alarm Goodridge. It was only much later when I began to do the dishes, with one hand in the sink and the other lifting a pot from the stove, that a current shot through me and I leapt several feet in the air. An electrician had to be summoned and finally found that the power intake had fused to the ground wire in the stove, which was not properly grounded. Such episodes were not conducive to a peaceful rehabilitation.

With all Montrealers we rejoiced as much as we could in the summer of 1967 in Expo, the World's Fair. The Canadian Pavilion took "Studio Window in Winter" from its place over our couch to hang in their Canadian art exhibit. We took Timothy to visit the fair, but the disastrous loss of his candied apple falling off its stick into the dirt and producing endless tears, seemed very much in tune with the vicissitudes we were experiencing in those days.

In 1968 with the addition of another cabin on the island in Georgian Bay, we were able to share it with my brother John and his wife Helen, whose presence provided security for both of us. We had not been back to stay at our island since the abortive effort in 1963. This time Goodridge was able to paint in relative calm as long as I did not leave the island except to go swimming where he could see me. I found this very difficult and was as restive as if I had been on a leash. One morning we awoke to what Goodridge felt was a smell of leaking propane from the kitchen stove. Our guests and I tried to reassure him by offering to light it to prove all was well. When the oven door blew off, we all agreed that this time his fears were totally justified.

Late in the '60s the National Gallery of Canada, then under the direction of Jean Sutherland Boggs, invited Goodridge to hold a one-man exhibition of his work. This was an incredible honour. In the preface of the catalogue, Jean Boggs says, "In deciding to give Goodridge Roberts one of the rare retrospective exhibitions the National Gallery devotes to living artists we have done so for the very consistency of his vision and because quite unselfconsciously it seems so particularly Canadian." Goodridge felt very pleased on the one hand and increasingly anxious on the other, since it seemed to symbolize the end of his career. Jim Borcoman was in charge of preparations at the Gallery and Alfie Pinsky, Chair of Fine Arts at Sir George Williams University (later to become Concordia University) where he became Dean of Fine Arts, was recruited to write a biographical sketch for the catalogue and to search out works in Montreal and photograph them for possible exhibition. Robert Ayre, art critic for the *Montreal Star* as well as a friend, also wrote an essay on the work included in the catalogue.

Shortly after we arrived at the farm in the late spring of 1969, Alfie began taping interviews with Goodridge about his life. Several times a week Goodridge would go over to Alfie's studio in the barn at our joint farm property and try to wrack his brains about what happened when, for Alfie to record on tape. The electroshock treatments made this exceedingly hard for him because of the associated memory loss. Alfie was naturally aware of the problem but I guess felt he had no alternative with the exhibition looming in the near future. It began to feel as if this forthcoming exhibition was a burden as much as a privilege and an honour. When it opened in Ottawa in late 1969, to be followed by showings in Montreal, Charlottetown, Hamilton, Québec City, and London, Ontario, Goodridge was far from his normal self and seemed to derive little pleasure from the event. His medication made him so like a zombie that it broke my heart, but I could do little except dissemble, fill in the gaps when possible and hope that the dissonance would not be as apparent to others as it was to me.

In a few months the exhibit came to Montreal, our "home town," where it had a special meaning. Whether pure happenstance or not, the Montreal Museum of Fine Arts managed to display the works in a way that could only be considered insulting. All 146 works were crammed into one large room on the ground floor, hung four or five deep without regard for any aesthetic considerations. It shocked the Montreal arts community; there were letters to the newspapers and a number of people whom we knew gave up their membership to the Museum. It seemed cruel and hurt Goodridge very much, and would have done so even if he had not been in such a vulnerable state.

The next year, 1970, a further honour occurred. Goodridge was made a Member (later an Officer) of the Order of Canada. We went to Ottawa for the investiture by Governor General Roland Michener at Rideau Hall. It was a solemn affair, but regrettably we were not able to receive much gratification from it. Nor was Goodridge able to do any painting to speak of in those days. Between 1969 and his death in 1974 his doctors felt he must paint in order to recover but, although he was inclined to believe the opposite was more likely, he tried to conform and on a couple of day-hospital admissions at the Allan, he was released at noon to come home and paint. At least this was more dignified than the humiliation he experienced earlier when he was in fulltime hospital care and had been sent to the Occupational Therapy Department in the hospital to paint. At home he would dash off a small still life as rapidly as possible to fulfill the commitment, but it always seemed as though were he to take his

Governor General Roland Michener presenting Goodridge with the
Order of Canada, Rideau Hall, Ottawa, April 21, 1970.

attention off the potential dangers in his environment for even the
shortest period, they would overwhelm him. However, some of these
cursorily produced paintings, which gave him much torment to
produce, nevertheless turned out well. More and more my role had
to shift from being a facilitator to actually initiating and carrying
out tasks relating to his work, whether it be purchasing paint,
receiving dealers, or photographing paintings. It was all part of sharing his life.

The years unfolded but recovery eluded him. Diagnoses were
changed with different doctors, medications switched, but to no avail.
It was almost beyond believing, as well as beyond bearing, that this
recently vital and vibrant man was in this deteriorated state. I was
working at my desk at Dawson College in January of 1974 when the
telephone rang and I was told by the hospital that he had developed
pneumonia and I should come very soon, but I barely had time to
gather my things together when another call informed me that he

had died so it was useless to hurry. Despite the preparation I had had for this moment, I was both shattered and relieved.

Some parts of the past are not remembered as a narrative but as a series of unconnected images, rather like vivid snapshots. Thus I remember the loving helpfulness of dear friends like Betty Ann Affleck who let us talk in her kitchen for hours, of Fred Poland who attended to autopsy and funeral arrangements, of Betty MacNeill who took me to the crematorium and also gave an eye to my wardrobe. There was music to arrange and speakers to contact as well as family. I remember going to St. George's School to pick up twelve-year-old Tim and to let him know. Funerals are supposed to be helpful and perhaps this one was, in its way. I felt comforted by the knowledge that others loved him too. I remember snatching the Order of Canada medal off the top of the coffin at the end before it could begin its journey to the crematorium. The many letters that poured in subsequently with tributes from people both known and unknown to me were a kind of solace. The strangest of these, though, was from Marian, Goodridge's first wife, who effectively thanked me for taking him on, saying that her own years with him had been enough, she couldn't take more. I didn't know whether to laugh or cry at this attempt to offer sympathy.

CHAPTER SEVENTEEN

Aftermath

FOR MANY YEARS after Goodridge died, surrounded as I was by his work and nourished by it, it seemed almost as if he continued to be present, as though he had just stepped out of the room for the moment. This was probably accentuated by the preceding years when he had so often been in hospital for short or long periods. Nevertheless I did mourn my loss of him, though certainly much of my grieving had already happened while he was still alive. As time went on I was able to be selective consciously or unconsciously, about which parts of him I kept alive and which parts I let go. The pain of his last years slipped away slowly as new demands surfaced.

In the first year Max Stern mounted a memorial exhibition at the Dominion Gallery of about ten of our paintings with a number that belonged to the gallery. Prices had to be set, based now on the knowledge that the supply was finite and there would be no new ones. Dealing with the work is an ongoing requirement when an artist is well-known and can persist for a very long time. The government requirements to settle the estate were a formidable first task needing a complete inventory of all the artwork and then certification by an expert, in our case Max Stern. I was concerned about how to proceed in the future best interests of my family. Max offered to buy everything, lock, stock, and barrel for what I remember to be a million or maybe a million and a half dollars. Knowing Max only too well I felt sure it wasn't enough, but more than that were the implications of divesting myself totally of what had been so important to me. They were all that was left of Goodridge and I could not bear the thought of losing them too.

For a number of years we had had an informal arrangement with Roberts Gallery (no relation) in Toronto that they would be our sole dealer in Toronto. They had built up a sizable market, selling in Ontario and the West. They were buying a lot from us. Jack Wildridge and his wife Jennie would visit at the farm or the city after a summer or winter of painting and pick out their choices. Through the '60s and early '70s they bought more than any other dealer did each year. Jack was a pleasure to deal with, organized, up-to-date with correspondence and payment, prepared to raise prices when appropriate and never asking to receive more than one-third of the selling price. I notice in my old files that in 1972 he was addressing his letters to me since Goodridge was in hospital and prior to that a number of letters were headed to both Goodridge and Joan, so it seems that my assuming responsibility for marketing the work had really begun before Goodridge's death. Roberts Gallery also mounted a memorial exhibition in 1975 and had subsequent exhibitions as well. I began, by 1978, to feel that too many of the best were getting sold for too little and that a different approach from that of a living artist was needed to handle the estate. I decided not to work only with Roberts Gallery in Toronto at that period. From time to time there continued to be issues which required important decisions about how to proceed in handling the paintings. Another Toronto dealer wanted to be able to buy as much as they desired exclusively and I rejected that offer, feeling that everything would be gone very quickly. It was not easy and probably I did not always make the best decision.

There was also the public gallery realm to consider. In 1975 the National Gallery put together the large exhibition "Canadian Painting in the Thirties" with Charles Hill's excellent catalogue. It was opened by the Prime Minister, Pierre Elliott Trudeau, and I felt I should go and do what I could to maintain the continuity and keep Goodridge's memory and work in the forefront of the art world's consideration. When I was introduced to Trudeau, and he said he had just seen me in a picture further down the wall, I disabused him and told him it was Marian, Goodridge's first wife. Then he asked me how things were in Québec now. Actually Québec was on the verge of electing its first Parti Québécois government, with unknown consequences. I really wanted to know what he thought, but I knew he would have to avoid answering any direct question. My solution was to say that I thought I would not vote at all, that it seemed like a useless exercise at the moment. He was insistent and repeated several times that I must vote. For him casting a vote, not the party, was the issue, and I admired his attitude. Of course I did vote.

Glynnis had a brief summer job with the Agnes Etherington Art Centre at Queen's University, finding, photographing, and documenting all the Roberts drawings that could be located. This was followed by a drawing exhibition there with a catalogue by Michael Bell. Also gratifying was the Art Gallery of Ontario Extension Department's project with Elke Town curating an exhibition of paintings from the '50s and '60s. Elke wrote a small catalogue with a few colour reproductions and the exhibition circulated through smaller Ontario cities.

Paintings were in group shows both at home and abroad. I particularly remember a Canadian art showing at the Tate Gallery in London, and Karen Wilkin showing Canadian art in New York City at the Borgenicht Gallery. We were told that John Candy was very interested in a particular Roberts, but in the end he did not acquire it. In the west we put together an exhibit in Edmonton at a private gallery in the late '70s and late in 1981 the Mendel Gallery in Saskatoon, with Karen Wilkin curating, mounted another exhibition with a colour catalogue entitled "Goodridge Roberts: Selected Works". It is pleasing indeed to have a critic of her stature on one's side, even if her support for the once pre-eminent American critic, Clement Greenberg, is now controversial.

In 2005 the City of Westmount placed Goodridge on its honour roll of citizens who have lived in Westmount and brought honour to it by their activities in the wider world in many spheres. For the *vin d'honneur* awards ceremony in Victoria Hall Tim and I prepared a booth with various mementoes, photographs, and memorabilia. Glynnis gave a brief speech about her step-father. It was well attended by many friends and was altogether a moving and satisfying evening. We were escorted home by a Public Security Officer's vehicle, much to the astonishment of our landlord!

After another twenty years or so of dealing with all the business matters involved with the paintings, I felt I wanted to do other things with the rest of my life and was relieved to turn over marketing and sales to Tim, whose knowledge and interest in the art world had progressed considerably from the day at four years of age when he had rushed into the studio where a dealer was discussing prices with me. In his hand he had a crayon drawing from nursery school and he said to her, "You can have this for twenty-five cents!" He had worked on and off at a couple of private galleries and also helped to hang and dismantle exhibitions at the Concordia University Art Gallery. In the '80s he opened a gallery on Sherbrooke Street with an older partner who failed to invest his half share of the start-up costs before disappearing and leaving Tim with the balance of a ten-year lease on their premises. When the downturn of the economy occurred at the beginning of the '90s, Tim's gallery closed. In 1999 a company named Terreverts Fine Arts was formed with Tim as president, and Goodridge's remaining paintings rolled into it for tax reasons. This pretty well ended my involvement in sales of the work, though on occasion I have had to show work to people who know me. It has been both a godsend economically and a burden caring for them.

There were inevitably other art-related matters in those years. Hugues de Jouvancourt, a writer and publisher of art books, decided to do a very expensive limited edition book on Goodridge Roberts with numbered copies, good colour reproductions, cloth covered and with beautiful paper. He had a good track record, having put out similar books on other Québec painters. We worked together finding and choosing appropriate works, and launched it at Tim's gallery.

Another different task occurred when we learned a painting was being marketed as a Roberts by a local restorer that Tim and I both felt was a fake. The issue went to court and the owner of the disputed painting hired an expert witness who was a sessional fine arts lecturer at Concordia. Tim and I were the opposing experts. We were delighted that the judge agreed with our testimony but I doubt we made any new friends with this venture. Subsequently, a number of fakes have shown up on the market which Tim follows up and exposes as inauthentic. The police are now much more vigilant and have greater capacity in the area of art fraud, fortunately.

Interest in Goodridge's work has continued and is spread widely throughout the country. The crowning glory in this regard was the 1998-99 retrospective exhibition entitled "Goodridge Roberts Revealed" at the McMichael Gallery in Kleinburg, Ontario, which travelled to Montreal, Québec City, Fredericton, and London, Ontario. Sandra Paikowsky, professor of art history at Concordia University and editor of the *Journal of Canadian Art History*, was the curator and produced a superb catalogue. The research was impeccable; the writing was lucid and understandable and added much to the pleasure of the exhibition. We both regretted that there were insufficient funds for it to be translated into French. There were 146 works shown, all reproduced in colour in the catalogue. Goodridge would have been so pleased. I think it was Sandra's tribute to an artist whose work both she and her husband, the painter John Fox, had loved for a long time and whom she respected as an artist.

The urn with Goodridge's ashes had been buried in the ground under the black cherry tree at the farm after his funeral. Glynnis, Tim, and myself were present, each with our own thoughts. When we left the farm for good in 1998, two years before Alfie Pinsky's death, it was a day of pouring rain, and our efforts to locate the urn after twenty-four years of growth in the underbrush were unsuccessful. Tim finally scooped up some earth with the shovel from what we concluded had to be very near the actual grave and put it in a plastic bag. That summer we laid to rest his final remains, or what passed for them, in the water just off our island in Georgian Bay, feeling Goodridge would prefer that to a property that was no longer ours. That, too, is now gone, but his spirit, certainly, is in his work there and in many other places with the many people who love it.

CHAPTER EIGHTEEN

My Life Continues

As GOODRIDGE's ILLNESS dragged on during the early 1970s, I could not help wondering if my life was not also drawing to a close and whether I would have any time left. As it has happened, I have been unbelievably grateful to have had thirty-five years with reasonably good health since his death in 1974. Since then my life has been work, play, and maintenance activities, like that of most people. I have not felt the desire to remarry. I know that for me, Goodridge could never be replaced. Glynnis, whom I have now been close to for many years, has always been so important to me. With her husband Robert they have given me two grandchildren whom I dearly love and who have now grown to adulthood. Tim continues his work with Goodridge's art as well as that of other painters. Too many beloved friends have died, as did my brother from lung cancer in his early sixties, and then my sister in 2008, at the age of ninety, from a stroke. She lives on, though, in her many family members, my fine nieces and nephews and their children.

Paid work, apart from everything else, was a strategy for survival when Goodridge was ill. It was possible to quickly enter another world away from personal problems, even if it was not always easy to keep them separated. I have had interesting and varied work but sometimes I thought I would have preferred a different profession. Early in my life with Goodridge I considered architecture, but found the gaps in my science and math background would be too hard to fill in order to qualify for the necessary education. Since Jacknife

159

days when we started with a how-to-build-a-house-book, I have been interested in houses and their design, an interest enhanced by friends. Ed Percival, of earlier chapters, was a civil engineer who built two different homes for his family, and whose daughter Ann is an architect. The architect Ray Affleck was a close friend until his death in 1989. He both encouraged and advised me in a dome-build-ing project I worked on for several years in the '70s. With its multi-coloured plexiglass panels it was perhaps more successful as a sort of sculpture on the island rocks than as an abode, but it was fun nonetheless, and I was able to spend the odd night or two sleeping in it.

I persevered in my chosen profession, but my career path took some unusual twists and turns. In 1964, when Tim was still very young, I was recovering from major operations in 1963 and 1964, and Goodridge had become ill, I felt I had to find part-time work to save my own sanity. I had left my job as field instructor for the McGill School of Social Work at the Allan Memorial Institute after Tim arrived, but I was able to land a half-time job doing demographic research with the Urban Social Redevelopment Project operating out of the University Settlement. This morphed into a survey of the social and mental health problems of the population in the area and then into the Mental Health Project under Dr. Raymond Prince. It was a bilingual psychiatric home treatment program with psychia-trists, social workers, and psychiatric residents. We issued our results in desktop publications. The work was stimulating and I enjoyed it, despite having to juggle it with keeping up a home, caring for a small child, and managing baby-sitters and a husband who was anxious and agitated. As one coping strategy, I made up a mimeographed list of everything we ever ate and then I just had to tick the items for the sitter to do the weekly grocery shopping.

In 1970 I received a telephone call while I was still at Georgian Bay on holiday, with a plea to become the acting director of the University Settlement. The newly hired director had managed to create huge turmoil in the agency. He had fired staff and was in turn

[top]Back row: Betty Ann Affleck, Joan, and Kay Percival.
Front row: Ed Percival and Ray Affleck, 1987.
[bottom] Architect Ray Affleck advised Joan on her multi-coloured
dome-building project.

fired himself. I considered it carefully and made it a condition of my acceptance that the fired staff would be reinstated, which I considered a necessity if peace was to be restored. When it was accepted, I agreed to come for a year. A very challenging year ensued with the potential for explosion never far away. A policy had been adopted which encouraged the citizens to run all their programs, the clothing depot, the handicraft workshop, the welfare recipients' group, the activist Milton-Park Citizen's Committee, and others, taking over this function from the professional service-givers. Trained community organizers supplied by the Settlement helped them in this work. For me, this was the first job where I had not been under the umbrella of someone of higher status, which added to the stress of the job. I thought some of my discomfort might stem from all those years when I had been number two while my sister was the boss. Long, contentious meetings at the board level, and especially with the coordinating committee, were part of the landscape. I did not want to have the job permanently after the year was up, despite it being offered to me, and eventually a permanent director was hired.

It was a relief to go on to a full-time teaching position at Dawson College in 1971. CEGEPs were new in Quebec and two-year-old Dawson was imbued with ideas of innovation, creativity, and commitment. I remember Paul Gallagher, the director general, telling teachers they should be prepared to burn out in five years after giving their all and then move onto another job. I was quite happy to remain in my teaching and administrative post as elected chairperson of the Social Service Department until 1980. We had established a new sort of program with "labs"—a couple of rented apartments based in the community where the students studied and worked with their teachers instead of being in classrooms. This program flourished for about eight years and was buttressed by a concurrent three-year action research evaluation study conducted by Margaret Westley, a sociologist. Its success depended on the hiring of creative teachers who were fully supportive of the changes and prepared to do a bit more. It also required acceptance from the Québec Provincial Committee for social service programs because, in combining courses, we were not following bureaucratic guidelines. We thought we could do it bilingually as well, which was too ambitious a challenge.

I have not talked about the Quiet Revolution and the profound economic, social, and political changes which Québec was undergoing in the '60s and '70s not because they did not affect us. Most anglophones, I think, just went on living their lives, deeply concerned, and desperately hoping that the country would not be split apart, feeling that no good would result from that but almost beyond talking about it any more as if it were like a fatal illness. Some were politically active on one side or the other. Others, myself among them, felt we might have been separatists if we had been francophone, because we were very aware of the injustices the Québécois had endured. But we also wondered if it would have been possible in the crunch for an anglophone to be included, no matter how bilingual. We awaited the results of both referendums (in 1980 and 1995) with bated breath.

After the close outcome of 1995 when separation was rejected by a mere hair's breadth, life slowly returned to a new normalcy for most anglophones.

After I left Dawson College in 1990 I developed a small private practice under the informal eye of a couple of more experienced psychotherapists. Referrals were all by word of mouth. For about ten years I worked with around fifty people, mostly women, who were trying to cope with personal dilemmas. I could control both my hours of work and the number of referrals I accepted. Also, I charged only what people could afford, which increased my satisfaction.

I also did some work trying to improve the functioning of several organizations. I was operating mostly on intuition because literature about the process of developing change in organizations was lacking, but I found that a good starting point was letting each

163

member in the group vent their feelings to me in private.

Together with Linda Davies, a graduating student in our program, we worked with a women's centre and a woman's shelter and then I was asked to tackle a science department at Dawson. If the Career Program co-ordinator had not left the college, we might have done more of this work which was both useful and satisfying.

"Fixing", or trying to fix, seems to be what I have gravitated to throughout my life. Perhaps that partly explains why Tim has ended up with a great variety of construction skills. I certainly admired the few "Renaissance" men I've known over the years who were seemingly capable of anything and everything. For me, this ideal of broad abili-ties has often been counterbalanced with its opposite, the excellence and depth within a narrower field which Goodridge typified.

My final paid employment came after I thought I had retired for good, but I was asked to take on the job of acting director for a social agency which was a home for single mothers and their babies. I agreed to do it for three months but again it took longer to sort out the pertinent issues and find a permanent director.

For recreation I found that my passion for competitive tennis began too late in my life for real achievement but lasted for the twenty years that I indulged it on different teams and groups in Montreal and Georgian Bay. Canoe trips in Algonquin Park and on Georgian Bay were always greatly enjoyed, a love shared by Kay and Ed from earliest days and then by Glynnis as well. Tim had other passions and my most vivid memory of him on a canoe trip is of Glynnis and me paddling with all our strength down a windswept channel while Tim sat in the middle engrossed in a new Hardy Boys book, oblivious to both the landscape and our struggle.

It has always been important for me to travel and spend time together as a family away from usual routines. It was the early way Glynnis and I reconnected, first in Barbados, then in 1975 on a month's visit to Greece with both Tim and Glynnis, and still later

Joan in her apartment with painting shown at Expo 67.
Montreal, circa 2002.
Photo: Janine Gauvreau

Tim with pickerel caught near Turning Island, not far from Bonnie Isle.

Left to right: Glynnis' husband Robert French,
daughter Lliana, Glynnis, and son Evan.

with Glynnis and Robert and their children, Evan and Lliana,
inBarbados and Florida. Other people sometimes travel to remote
places to have respite from family pressures, but for me it was the
reverse. It was a way to try and heal wounds, to knit us together.

Summers continued to be Georgian Bay and the island with
those who loved it and who returned year after year. In 1977 we ran
a windsurfing school at the island with Glynnis as expert instructor
and Tim as bookkeeper and rescuer of stranded pupils. Later Tim
converted the island to solar power for lighting, water pumps, and
radios. We could not resolve the problem of what would happen
after my death with the children's differing lifestyles. In addition,
due to the growing affluence of the area, rising prices and taxes
became a concern. Toronto residents could come and go but with
an eight-hour drive we Montrealers could not. Being there alone
would only become more difficult for me as the years passed. Selling
became the only solution, much as it was very painful for all of us.
The island went to new owners in 2006, nearly one hundred years
since my father first went on a canoe trip there as a young law student.

It is not easy to account for the breadth of topics which I have pursued over the years through courses of many kinds offered by many different sponsors. I have been involved with four universities in the province, two seniors' organizations, the Visual Arts Centre, the Montreal Power Squadron, and the Protestant School Board of Greater Montreal (now the English School Board). How could I possibly have been interested in both nautical navigation and translation from Spanish to English, in both graphology and *droit constitutionnel*? I can only say it happened and I was.

As I reflect on my life it seems that many things I thought were important have slipped to the periphery while the main focus, the central core of my life, has been Goodridge. There were so many things I would not have experienced or learned if I had not known him. Without him my life would have been more prosaic, less demanding, less stimulating, but also less exciting and less rich in so many ways. It would have been a duller, less inspired life, and doors of all kinds would not have opened for me. There would likely have been less laughter and fun. In the jumble and everyday trivialities of living, Goodridge continues to be present for me and to inspire and occupy my ongoing life. I miss him to this day and I wish we could have had a longer time together to enjoy and explore our partnership.

1960.

Index

Véhicule Press

www.vehiculepress.com